Y0-BDF-761

Animus Aeternus

Marie-Louise von Franz, Honorary Patron

**Studies in Jungian Psychology
by Jungian Analysts**

Daryl Sharp, General Editor

ANIMUS AETERNUS

Exploring the Inner Masculine

Deldon Anne McNeely

Also by Deldon Anne McNeely in this series:
Touching: Body Therapy and Depth Psychology (title 30, 1987)

Canadian Cataloguing in Publication Data

McNeely, Deldon Anne
    Animus aeternus

(Studies in Jungian psychology by Jungian analysts; 49)

Includes bibliographical references and index.

ISBN 0-919123-50-3

1. Animus (Psychoanalysis).
2. Women—Psychology.
3. Imagery (Psychology)—Therapeutic use.
4. Poetry—Psychological aspects.
5. Women poets—Psychology.
6. Jung, C.G. (Carl Gustav), 1875-1961.
I. Title. II. Series.

BF175.5.A53M26 1991   150.19'54   C90-095914-2

Copyright © 1991 by Deldon Anne McNeely.
All rights reserved.

INNER CITY BOOKS
Box 1271, Station Q, Toronto, Canada M4T 2P4
Telephone (416) 927-0355
FAX 416-924-1814

Honorary Patron: Marie-Louise von Franz.
Publisher and General Editor: Daryl Sharp.
Senior Editor: Victoria Cowan.

INNER CITY BOOKS was founded in 1980 to promote the
understanding and practical application of the work of C.G. Jung.

Cover: Man with Three Masks, by Lee Lawson (© 1990).

Index by Daryl Sharp

Printed and bound in Canada by John Deyell Company

Contents

See last page for descriptions of other Inner City Books

Preface

Not in stubbornness but in humility, I refused to write for so long
that I felt pressed down under the whip of God into a bed of sickness.
... Beaten down by many kinds of illnesses, I put my hand to writing. Once I did this, a deep and profound exposition of books came
over me. I received the strength to rise up from my sick bed, and under that power I continued to carry out the work to the end.
                    —Hildegard of Bingen, *Scivias.*

The purpose of this work is to share something of my explorations
and excavations, and similar searchings of friends and patients. We
try to see and feel all we can of our lives, and Life, and the relationship between the sexes, especially as that relationship is reflected in
the poetry of women.

Many people have been with us in this work, helping to focus the
lenses and the lights, the natural radiance of the sun, the reflected
cyclical moonlight and the Promethean lamps. Others, by their sensi-
tivity to touch where touch is needed, and to music, the great opener,
have enabled us to reach feelings which might have remained dor-
mant. Speaking for myself, I would like to acknowledge that many
men are among them, men who have touched and opened me
through their example, their poetry, their nurturance and love. I
thank them all, fathers, sons, husbands, brothers, lovers, teachers,
therapists, spiritual advisors, friends, artists. There are countless poems written by men that are brilliantly relevant to this process, for it
is not just a woman's work. However, I made the decision to include
here only the poetry of women.

Appreciation is gratefully extended to the writers and poets represented here, and to those many wonderful women whose influence
has stimulated me. Special thanks to Gayonne Goodyear, Judy
Andry and the women's seminar in New Orleans, and to Regina
Meadows and Harvey Rifkin for listening seriously.

My aim has been to proceed in the spirit of Edna St. Vincent
Millay, whose creative drive for clarity is reflected in this sonnet:

7

I will put Chaos into fourteen lines
And keep him there; and let him thence escape
If he be lucky; let him twist, and ape
Flood, fire, and demon—his adroit designs
Will strain to nothing in the strict confines
Of this sweet Order, where, in pious rape,
I hold his essence and amorphous shape,
Till he with Order mingles and combines.
Past are the hours, the years, of our duress,
His arrogance, our awful servitude:
I have him. He is nothing more nor less
Than something simple not yet understood;
I shall not even force him to confess;
Or answer. I will only make him good.[1]

---

[1] *Collected Poems,* sonnet clxviii, p. 728.

1

Introduction

Of all Jung's concepts, that of the syzygy or contrasexual archetypes, anima and animus, excites some of the liveliest debate, intro-
ducing both confusion and fascination among contemporary theo-
rists. This is due in part to the rapidly changing place of the feminine
in the collective unconscious, in part to Jung's personality and his
own blindspots in regard to the individuation process in women, and
also to the innate elusiveness of archetypal energies. These three
factors interact to produce great movements of energy around the
terms Jung took from the Latin: *anima,* literally "soul," and *animus,*
literally "mind" (also spirit, courage and anger).

They are both personal and collective, always present though fun-
damentally connected to the past. Bigger than life, they yet occupy
the minutiae of our most mundane moments, hiding in our lovers and
relatives and exposing themselves when most inconvenient. They
lead us down worldly dead-ends and seduce us guilelessly into internal labyrinths. Anima and animus maintain their stride despite the
storms, ecstasy and heartbreak in their wake.

Because archetypal energies manifest through our deepest drives
and desires and through images that societies accept as "reality," the
flow of experience between biological urges and cultural influences
creates a continual movement in their expression. Looking at these
three sources of confusion in terms of the syzygy makes it clear why
one man's attempt to describe the phenomena of contrasexuality
would prove to be a heroic undertaking subject to strong reactions.

The changing place of the feminine in the collective unconscious is
now unmistakable. Differences in behavior and images regarding
woman's lifestyle continue to emerge. Led by affluent Western societies where biological realities can at times be superceded—through
contraception, medicine, communication systems and other techno-
logical developments—the concept of the reality of woman's world
has been radically altered.

Paradoxically, the patriarchy's orientation to nature—its emphasis on the manipulation of natural resources—has made it possible for the outcry of "Enough!" to be taken up and heard. It is woman who has been freed of her biological constraints through technology, and it is woman who leads the way in calling a halt to the rape of earth's natural resources.

> Woman dancing with hair
> on fire, woman writhing in the
> cone of orange snakes, flowering
> into crackling lithe vines:
> Woman
> you are not the bound witch
> at the stake, whose broiled alive
> agonized screams
> thrust from charred flesh
> darkened Europe in the nine millions.
> Woman
> you are not the madonna impaled
> whose sacrifice of self leaves her
> empty and mad as wind,
> or whore crucified
> studded with nails.
>
> Woman
> you are the demon of a fountain of energy
> rushing up from the coal hard
> memories in the ancient spine,
> flickering lights from the furnace in the solar
> plexus, lush scents from the reptilian brain,
> river that winds up the hypothalamus
> with its fibroids of pleasure and pain
> twisted and braided like rope,
> firing the lanterns of the forebrain
> till they glow blood red.
>
> You are the fire sprite
> that charges leaping thighs,
> that whips the supple back on its arc
> as deer leap through the ankles:
> dance of a woman strong
> in beauty that crouches

inside like a cougar in the belly
not in the eyes of others measuring.

You are the icon of woman sexual
in herself like a great forest tree
in flower, liriodendron bearing sweet tulips,
cups of joy and drunkenness.
You drink strength from your dark fierce roots
and you hang at the sun's own fiery breast
and with the green cities of your boughs
you shelter and celebrate
woman, with the cauldrons of your energies
burning red, burning green.[2]

Piercy evokes the power of the feminine accepted by woman as her own, after centuries of projecting it upon men, who responded by demonizing those women who did not project it. The evil one with snakey-locks can now be seen as a fruitful one, growing vines, and the sexuality that once made her a devil is now a source of celebration. No longer depending on others to evaluate her worth, she feels her own value; the caldrons, once a symbol of her witchy projection, are now the seat of creative fire.

Much has been written about how Jung's personal psychology influenced his thinking and his values. From our current standpoint, we can see his blind spots. But Jung had the courage to say what he saw, and also to encourage those who followed to do the same, rather than be bound to his thought as dogma. Because he wrote from the perspective of a culture dominated by gender stereotypes, Jung's ideas reflect a certain amount of stereotyping, despite the fact that he struggled to be fair and objective. He presented his sexual dichotomy as symbolic, acknowledging that aspects of animus and anima, especially in terms of Logos and Eros, respectively, may be found in both males and females. He expected them to be found in different degrees of development in each. Times have changed and gender roles have changed. What is eternally enduring about sexuality is yet to be delineated.

The following poem, spun off from a woman's dream, reflects the

---

2 Marge Piercy, "The Window of the Woman Burning," *Circles on the Water,* pp. 202-203.

dreamer's relationship to Jung as an animus figure onto which she projects the generative father, as many women have done.

> Carl Jung, whose name means "young"
> restored to me a part of myself.
> In gratitude i sat,
> skirtless, on his lap,
> he an old man on the river (but did he feel young!)
> his clothing white and newly changed.
> I was shy
> but laid my cheek on his
> as i fondled his
> yellow crystal necklace.
> He told me it was leather,
> not crystal.
> He told me with his smile
> that my mother and i are sisters
> but our eros natures have
> hair of different waves,
> then indicated the interview was over,
> it was time to feed the dogs,
> time for us all to prepare for the journey[3]

The images in the poem of regeneration and rebirth, and the juxtapositioning of youth and old age, prepare the dreamer for a new relationship with both the feminine images she has inherited and her own instinctual way.

And now the third factor: direct knowledge of the nature of archetypes is out of the scope of human endeavor; that should keep us humble. The puzzling issues evoked by a male/female dichotomy were not invented by Jung. Animus/anima will not go away if we just ignore them. The goddess of vegetation will be known; she will not remain buried under the cathedral forever. Neither will mankind (one aspect of humankind) submit to being forever under her thumb, green though it may be. The adventurous hero who aspires to shooting the moon will likely persevere, resisting attempts to convince him of his folly. The tensions between emanations of the Divine that play us like toys create ever moving chiaroscuros; what is now in the

---

3 Claudia E. Lapp, "Jung," *Cloud Gate,* p. 29.

darkness may tomorrow be in the light. This quality of change, eternally ongoing—physical, psychological and spiritual—is captured by Mary Oliver:

> We climbed through a broken window,
> walked through every room.
>
> Out of business for years,
> the mattresses held only
>
> rainwater, and one
> woman's black shoe. Downstairs
>
> spiders had wrapped up
> the crystal chandelier.
>
> A cracked cup lay in the sink.
> But we were fourteen,
>
> and no way dust could hide
> the expected glamour from us,
>
> or teach us anything.
> We whispered, we imagined.
>
> It would be years before
> we'd learn how effortlessly
>
> sin blooms, then softens,
> like any bed of flowers.[4]

In spite of the confusion and shortcomings entailed in the concept of the syzygy, it remains a viable and pragmatic concept in the practice of analysis. That is why many of us continue our efforts to understand and differentiate aspects of anima and animus, while others think in terms of genderless polarities, like soul and spirit, or Eros and Logos. In our present state of development in sexual relatedness, the image of the inner male and inner female is both psychologically appealing and useful. Though it is complicated, it is worth attempting to sort out that pairing in the individuation process. It is all but impossible not to project the contrasexual archetype. It is a natural response in relationships. The question is whether we understand what

---

4 "An Old Whorehouse," *American Primitive*, p. 39.

is happening. There is still much exploring to be done before we can avoid identifying others with these archetypes.[5]

For example, as I set out to write about the animus, I am moved to ask, where is he in this project? Does he motivate me to think about and define him? Does he fuel the writing itself? Does he need me to communicate my thoughts and feelings? Do I need him to be literate? Do I write about him in order to come to the Self or to meet some need for ego-recognition? Does he applaud or dissuade me, or both? Does he want me to be seen and heard in the world, or does he want me to focus exclusively on him, face turned toward the inner process alone?

While sometimes his voice is unmistakably clear, those times are rare. Often I am not sure where he is and what he wants. Sometimes he simply will not speak. During body movement he often disappears—perhaps overwhelmed by the feminine body presence.

Only in dreams do I find the animus unequivocally present in a consistent and communicative way, and then I discover something very interesting. If I write a poem derived from the aura of the dream, he not only appears but brings all sorts of additional information.

I once tried to describe a princely type of male who appeared in a dream by writing a poem about him.[6] He became exquisitely clear in the poem, and also explained the life history behind his narcissistic style. He laid out the family dynamics in a way which I had never thought about consciously, as if he had been in reductive analysis for several years! Suddenly it dawned on me that he did not want to be confronted directly, but wanted to be paid attention in an indirect and activity centered way, like many a shy man. I began to see poetry as an oblique approach which not only gave me information but apparently gave us both a lot of pleasure. Having found this to be consistently helpful, I encouraged it in women who showed an interest in writing; it worked for many of them as well.

In familiarizing analysands with the concept of the syzygy I ask them to imagine a contrasexual partner accompanying them through

---

[5] See Andrew Samuels, chapter 7, "Gender, Sex, Marriage," *Jung and the Post-Jungians,* pp. 207-229.

[6] This poem is presented in part in chapter 11.

life, but at a pace that is usually out of step with the conscious personality. If the ego is principally feminine, we look for the male within, knowing that he may be very different in developmental level, in values, interests, etc. But he wants to be acknowledged, wants to be conscious, wants to have his influence, and should be allowed to engage in dialogue with the conscious mind, as numerous Jungian writers have demonstrated.[7]

In his elucidation of the anima, James Hillman warns us that it can be detrimental to listen to anima's ploy, which would be to convince us to describe her only in vague terms because anima is necessarily diffuse.[8] Similarly I believe animus gives messages which defy our efforts to bring consciousness to him in a feminine mode. He would exhort us to continually clarify and refine, to the point of extreme discouragement and abandonment of the attempt. Yet, I see that women find it extremely helpful to write about their experience of the animus, especially when they are naive about Jungian concepts.

Matthew Fox states in his presentation of Hildegard's work that for a time she refused to write "because of doubt and erroneous thinking and because of controversial advice from men."[9] Overcoming this writer's block marked her spiritual awakening. In my personal experience such discouragement comes from within, particularly when writing for possible publication. Even when writing supports the positive animus, the discouragement appears to be sparked by the negative animus. It takes such forms as, "That has already been said," "It's not worth the trouble," and a number of corollaries, such as, "It won't be read," or "It will meet with nothing but criticism," and the most deadly of all: "It's impossible to put all that into any meaningful form."

In trying to write about animus, my mind begins to race through everything I have ever read or heard about him, like a giant computer search with no one at the terminal. There is a traffic jam of images, memories and especially criticisms suggesting that to sort all this out

---

7 See, for example, Barbara Hannah, *Encounters with the Soul: Active Imagination As Developed by C.G. Jung,* and Irene Claremont de Castillejo, *Knowing Woman: A Feminine Psychology.*

8 James Hillman, *Anima: An Anatomy of a Personified Notion,* pp. 1-5.

9 *Illuminations of Hildegard of Bingen,* p. 27.

would require a team of genies. Take cleaning up the kitchen after several children have made a meal for themselves and multiply the mess by, say, twenty, and you come close to the feeling-tone of the experience of making the decision to begin. It sometimes seems as if the only solution is to burn the kitchen (and by the way, leave writing to the men). In other words, as the anima says, "To describe me you must be obtuse," so the animus says, "To describe me you must be impossibly precise, nothing less than perfection will be adequate. Better go make bread."

Many female writers have described this problem. Virginia Woolf gave the destructive voice a feminine persona, calling it the "angel in the house," but the experience is the same. She wrote that her house-angel told her to "never let anybody guess that you have a mind of your own."[10] This "angel" is what Jung called an anima woman; her ego has no loyalty to the female sex, but is under the domination of the masculine principle.

It is likely that this relationship was modeled for Woolf by her mother and father. Though strong in her own right, Woolf's mother deferred and catered to her husband, the writer Leslie Stevens. When in Woolf's early adolescence her mother died an untimely death, her father became morbidly self-pitying, subject to outbursts of rage when his children did not accommodate to his moods. Woolf's elder sister bore the brunt of his demands, and had to exercise extraordinary fortitude in order to marry and live in her own home.

Woolf describes how she destroyed the "angel in the house" in order to find her own voice. But later in life Woolf killed again, this time drowning herself. What is the relationship between these two killings? I want to offer some information and understanding of the processes involved in such events.

Poet Glenda Taylor concedes to the animus' demand for being all inclusive by prefacing her work with the following:

> I speak, till you cry out
> "Partial! Only partial!"
> Then I go silent.
> I paint, but you say

---

10 "Professions for Women," *The Death of the Moth,* p. 151.

"One, only one of the limitless possible,"
and so I cease to paint.

I wish to publish, yet you whisper
"Ah, but you'll be penned to one perspective
and who will know you know there is
another side," so I sit, impotent,

Shackled by knowledge of Shiva's dance
of endless shifting forms
in which an any one is all,
but also none,

Until I promise you this preface
to fly, a flag of concession,
in the forefront of all my work,

Honoring the off-setting, never encompassed,
equally sacred, counterbalancing,
other side. Tao.[11]

Paula Bennett in her study of female creativity quotes Simone de Beauvoir on this subject of woman's unwillingness to be "displeasing" in writing. Bennett points out that prior to the 1960s, few women had the courage to express themselves freely as writers. But in the 60s, Adrienne Rich and others

picked up their loaded guns, and with a zeal unparalleled in women's history, they did everything Simone de Beauvoir said a woman lacked the courage to do; they investigated; they disarranged; above all, they exploded.[12]

Now, in the 90s, the problem is not so much one of courage, nor of finding an audience, but, as Marge Piercy puts it, of "unlearning to not speak." This is a problem with the inner man, and can only be resolved by inner work.

Blizzards of paper
in slow motion
sift through her.
In nightmares she suddenly recalls

---

11 "In Honor of That Not Spoken," *Life Is a River*, p. ii.
12 *My Life a Loaded Gun*, p 242.

a class she signed up for
but forgot to attend.
Now it is too late.
Now it is time for finals:
losers will be shot.
Phrases of men who lectured her
drift and rustle in piles:
Why don't you speak up?
Why are you shouting?
You have the wrong answer,
wrong line, wrong face.
They tell her she is womb-man,
babymachine, mirror-image, toy,
earth mother and penis-poor,
a dish of synthetic strawberry ice-cream
rapidly melting.
She grunts to a halt.
She must learn again to speak
starting with I
starting with We
starting as the infant does
with her own true hunger
and pleasure
and rage.[13]

Most women have known the experience of struggling through confusion to a clear insight into the relationship with a man; you screw up your courage to talk with him about it and . . . Presto! He disappears! He did not have the advantage of mustering courage; you have given him a surprise, which to him felt like a "surprise *attack,*" and he fled. The animus, or inner man, until we have been aware of him for a long time and worked to bring him to a point of conscious development, reacts just like an unconscious man in the outer world. Reacting like the person new to psychotherapy, he is defensive rather than curious about himself. Say, "I feel hurt by you," and he will not say, "I'm sorry; how have I hurt you?" More often he will argue that you should not feel hurt.

My personal response, after many years learning to relate to an-

---

13 "Unlearning to Not Speak," *Circles on the Water,* p. 97.

imus figures—both inner and outer—has been to go at them obliquely through my own favorite medium, poetry. Poetry when it's "on" has the authenticity of a lucid dream. I have had the experience of sharing a poem which was not appreciated, or was misunderstood, or disparaged in some hurtful way; nevertheless my attachment to the poem, if it carried truth for me, did not diminish. I may have decided to take it and hide out underground with it for a while, or forever, but I wouldn't discard it. In "Poem Gift," I described the feeling:

> I gave a friend a poem . . .
> he swallowed it whole.
> Nothing came back,
> nothing at all.
>
> Later he threw it up
> with someone who felt safe.
> Neither of them
> could digest it.
>
> Poetry is strong medicine.
> Someone said sin
> means missing the mark.
> Can a poem sin?
>
> A bullseye poem is holy,
> cuts through the fog,
> strikes the heart like a harp,
> and whoever can take it in
> knows love.

This is my subjective experience and I would not try to impose poetry on others as *the* way of active imagination. Katherine Bradway has described her use of sandplay to explore the animus.[14] Music, movement and art may also be important, both as forms of active imagination and in amplifying dreams. However, I think the concept of coming at the animus indirectly may speak to many women, and for some, coming at him poetically will be quite fruitful.

Often a poem comes in the form of a statement directed to the an-

---

14 "Gender Identity and Gender Roles: Their Place in Analytic Practice."

imus; sometimes he speaks through the woman and the poem has a masculine voice; sometimes the voice is that of an animus position reflected in the way the woman speaks about herself.

It is not my intention to present the poems in this book as literature, nor to place value judgments on what a good poem should be. Here we are concerned with the soul-making of the poet, not the art form. This poetry is about becoming whole, about knowing oneself and thereby empathizing with others.

Perhaps these poems will cut through some of the fog; perhaps some will even strike the harpstring in your heart. At the very least, they may demonstrate the usefulness of the concept of the animus. Admittedly, we will not here resolve all the confusion that surrounds the sexual dichotomy. But I hope to shed some clarity on a subject which may forever require more differentiation.

2

Unisex or Syzygy

Can we avoid subdividing people into male and female? Jung's belief, as demonstrated throughout his work and particularly in *Aion,* was that there is a universal tendency to perceive God as unfolding in the world in the form of paired opposites, such as male/female, day/night, yin/yang, etc. Though Jung has been criticized for setting up dualities, he was simply recording his observation of an all-pervasive tendency.

Eric Neumann's classic work, *The Origins and History of Consciousness,* describes consciousness in terms of archetypal stages reflected in both the collective and the individual. An important point of development is the separation of the World Parents, in which the germ of ego-consciousness asserts itself against its symbiotic attachment to the unconscious. In Neumann's concept the unconscious is personified as the Great Mother, and the creation of an ego is a masculine process. Neumann observed that the earliest conceptions of the world and the gods are created by us in our own image and are related to the body; therefore we image the birth of consciousness, of individuality, as a process of birth from a woman's body.

This seems reasonable, and mythological development bears out this relationship. Still, it is a concretization that avoids the recognition of the continuity of the coniunctio throughout being. The masculine is present in the creation of new life. And the developing ego does not act only assertively; it is also pushed, or it waits for the right moment, containing its yin energy.

Although Neumann's schema seems unnecessarily polarized between male and female, in some ways it has been quite useful in aiding our conceptualization of the individuation process. In the unconscious, in the consciousness of undeveloped persons and of young children, opposites do not exist. But after the separation of the World Parents is accomplished by the drive to consciousness, the psyche perceives the world in terms of polarities.

The inward as well as the outward development of culture begins with the coming of light and the separation of the World Parents. Not only do day and night, back and front, upper and lower, inside and outside, I and You, male and female, grow out of this development of opposites and differentiate themselves from the original promiscuity, but opposites like "sacred" and "profane," "good" and "evil," are now assigned their places in the world.[15]

Through the heroic act of world creation and division of opposites, the ego steps forth from the magic circle of the uroboros and finds itself in a state of loneliness and discord. With the emergence of the fully fledged ego, the paradisal situation is abolished; the infantile condition, in which life was regulated by something ampler and more embracing, is at an end, and with it the natural dependence on that ample embrace.[16]

This stage is identified in other theoretical models, though the descriptions and focus differ slightly. For example, there are the oral-aggressive through anal-expulsive stages in psychoanalytic drive theory, and in object relations theory the separation-individuation stage continues through the stage of rapprochement. Whatever the theory, it appears that the stage of psychic unity, or symbiosis, gives birth to the nascent ego by around the middle of the first year of life. Within the next two years the child becomes a psychological entity, and psychological hermaphroditism gives way to gender identity.

But what exactly does an infant discover in discriminating between male and female? Does it *learn* sexuality? Are the child's responses evoked by obvious cues of dress and voice, or the more subtle sexual emanations such as slight differences in odor, for example, that may be given off by hormonal changes, temperatures, moisture, etc.? Or do the psychological sexual characteristics unfold according to genetic coding?

My own belief is that we are much more affected by nature than nurture in this regard, and arrive in the world with a fairly secure set of instructions for development, which environmental factors can alter within parameters set by our constitutional make-up. Does a "true" feminine and masculine principle exist in nature apart from

---

15 *The Origins and History of Consciousness,* p. 109.
16 Ibid., p. 114.

human projection? This conundrum cannot be resolved in our present state of knowledge, but the evidence from our relationship to the animal world, from history, and the universality of sexual differentiation in human cultures suggests there is an abiding difference in masculine and feminine characteristics beyond those assigned by culture. Since human beings cannot be studied apart from culture, this cannot be proven.[17]

Theoretically, a unisex world could be created where no differences were obvious between the psychologies of men and women. My fantasy is that in this imagined unisexual world, some individual would experiment with differentiating him- or herself, and, because of the attractiveness of polarities, the opposition of male/female would simply begin again to unfold to its full polarization!

Androgyny means something other than hermaphroditism; the latter implies undifferentiated fusion, whereas androgyny implies well-differentiated integration. The androgyny of the individuated person allows for—one might even say depends upon—freedom of expression of contrasexual characteristics.

Jane Wheelwright notes:

> My contention is that the animus and anima are not consistently integrated except in old age. This means the self includes both femaleness and maleness equally. Therefore, I perceive androgyny as a self symbol, in the sense that we formerly used the hermaphrodite as a self symbol.[18]

If we accept Jung's view, then anima and animus exist beyond the realm of human consciousness as abiding structures of the psyche, which, though separate, form a pair. One cannot be activated without a concomitant movement in the other. In the psyche of each human being they dance in reciprocity. From this point of view the yin/yang duality is archetypal and therefore universally attractive. Edna St.Vincent Millay illustrates the cosmic syzygy imaginatively in these two sonnets:

---

17 See Carol Gilligan, *In a Different Voice,* for research into feminine identity formation; also Florence Wiedemann and Polly Young-Eisendrath, *Female Authority: Empowering Women Through Psychotherapy.*
18 *For Women Growing Older,* p. 7.

O Earth, unhappy planet born to die,
Might I your scribe and your confessor be,
What wonders must you not relate to me
Of Man, who when his destiny was high
Strode like the sun into the middle sky
And shone an hour, and who so bright as he,
And like the sun went down into the sea,
Leaving no spark to be remembered by.
But no; you have not learned in all these years
To tell the leopard and the newt apart;
Man, with his singular laughter, his droll tears,
His engines and his conscience and his art,
Made but a simple sound upon your ears:
The patient beating of the animal heart.[19]

His heatless room the watcher of the stars
Nightly inhabits when the night is clear;
Propping his mattress on the turning sphere,
Saturn his rings or Jupiter his bars
He follows, or the fleeing moons of Mars,
Till from his ticking lens they disappear . . .
Whereat he sighs, and yawns, and on his ear
The busy chirp of Earth remotely jars.
Peace at the void's heart through the wordless night,
A lamb cropping the awful grasses, grazed;
Earthward the trouble lies, where strikes his light
At dawn industrious Man, and unamazed
Goes forth to plow, flinging a ribald stone
At all endeavor alien to his own. [20]

These sonnets beautifully depict the separation of humankind from the World Parents. They also illustrate Millay's image of the detachment of Earth and Heaven from each other as well as from human beings. This kind of differentiation of cosmic forces is representative of a certain level of consciousness through which all healthy human beings proceed.

The mind develops through a process of continual differentiation and integration. In this sense, the capacity to think dualistically rep-

---

[19] *Collected Poems*, "Epitaph for the Race of Man," sonnet iv, p. 704.
[20] Ibid., sonnet xiii, p. 713.

resents an important step in early life. It can be conceptualized as an act of aggression, this severing of a whole into parts; that is the yang side of the experience. The yin side preserves the mutual relatedness of the parts as pieces of an original whole. Both are necessary for the developmental process to move forward. The stage of differentiation may last for a second, an hour or most of a lifetime before a reintegration occurs.

In the healthy infant's differentiation of the mother into a "good" and "bad" object, it is believed that reintegration occurs somewhere during the first year of life. Without the differentiation there will be serious disturbances in the ability to trust and relate to other people. The infant may remain passive and dependent, become paranoid or vacillate between seeing every close person as friend or enemy. If the process of differentiation is experienced and a reintegration of mother as a single object occurs, the infant acquires the marvellous capacity to see mother as a "good-enough" person.[21] Then any sense of frustration or loss resulting from her behavior can be perceived as temporary, not hopeless.

Where there is a "severing" of the state of hermaphroditism into perceptions of male and female, the reintegration to the androgynous stage can take a lifetime, and cannot be said to ever occur completely in the physical experience. The need to differentiate, to seek out the opposite and to come together, physically and symbolically, is the drama of life, the essence of preservation and germination.[22]

Marge Piercy reflects on the consequences and meaning of gender identity:

> The moon is always female and so
> am I although often in this vale
> of razorblades I have wished I could
> put on and take off my sex like a dress
> and why not? Do men wear their sex

---

[21] The "good-enough" mother refers to one who can accept the child's "gestures of omnipotence." The not-good-enough mother forces the child to accommodate to *her* gestures, which leads to the child's developing a "false self," sacrificing personal needs to those of the parents. See D.W. Winnicott, *The Maturational Process and the Facilitating Environment.*.

[22] For a discussion of facets of consciousness, see Andrew Samuels, *Jung and the Post-Jungians,* p. 59.

always? The priest, the doctor, the teacher
all tell us they come to their professions
neuter as clams and the truth is
when I work I am pure as an angel
tiger and clear is my eye and hot
my brain and silent all the whining
grunting piglets of the appetites.
For we were priests to the goddesses
to whom were fashioned the first altars
of clumsy stone on stone and leaping animal
in the wombdark caves, long before men
put on skirts and masks to scare babies.
For we were healers with herbs and poultices
with our milk and careful fingers
long before they began learning to cut up
the living by making jokes at corpses.
For we were making sounds from our throats
and lips to warn and encourage the helpless
young long before schools were built
to teach boys to obey and be bored and kill.
. . . .

I have wandered these chambers in the rock
where the moon freezes the air and all hair
is black or silver. Now I will tell you
what I have learned lying under the moon
naked as women do: now I will tell you
the changes of the high and lower moon.
Out of necessity's hard stones we suck
what water we can and so we have survived,
women born of women. There is knowing
with the teeth as well as knowing with
the tongue and knowing with the fingertips
as well as knowing with words and with all
the fine flickering hungers of the brain.[23]

It is the privilege of the integrated personality to be able to regress
to earlier states by decision. Michael Fordham includes in a list of

---

[23] From "The Moon Is Always Female," *The Moon Is Always Female,* pp. 91-94.

ego-functions the "capacity to relinquish its controlling and organizing functions."[24] The securely formed ego is able to permit the emergence of previously non-egoic aspects of the psyche. Early analysts referred to this as regression in the service of the ego.

Writers help us to imagine the state of fusion that exists before consciousness takes in duality. People often revert to this early ego state in analysis, at times of fatigue, or in celebration; for example, the permission to costume for special occasions—parties, Halloween, Mardi Gras—provokes many people to don a hermaphroditic disguise. In analysis people sometimes touch early experiences of sexual confusion and indecision, and recognize some of the ways in which they forged a sexual identity in infancy.

Denise Levertov describes intentional undifferentiation, the choosing of a mystical state of fusion with nature:

> The moon is a sow
> and grunts in my throat
> Her great shining shines through me
> so the mud of my hollow gleams
> and breaks in silver bubbles
>
> She is a sow
> and I a pig and a poet
>
> When she opens her white
> lips to devour me I bite back
> and laughter rocks the moon
>
> In the black of desire
> we rock and grunt, grunt and
> shine[25]

---

[24] *Children As Individuals*, pp. 93-96.

[25] "Song for Ishtar," in Richard Ellman and Robert O'Clair, eds., *The Norton Anthology of Modern Poetry*, p. 1063.

3

Animus and Ego

Animus, O Animus, wherefore art thou, Animus? Please step forward out of the shadows, out from behind the dark foliage which camouflages you, into the moonlight, and show yourself to be a true, substantial bridegroom.

Or must I play this scene alone, foolish in my belief that this soliloquy finds an audience? Alas, who speaks? Is it I or you? Aren't you the Word? The one who insists on clarity? So why am I out here alone on this balcony and you invisible? True, I'm the one who wants togetherness; perhaps by withholding yourself you flush me out so you can see *me* clearly. How do I get what I need from you? How do I even know what I need from you? You're supposed to be the assertive one. Am I at your mercy, waiting to be overtaken? And if you come, who in me stands up to you? Can you bear to look me in the eye, or must I feign indifference? Do you respond to honesty, or only to coyness, or, worse yet, must I treat you sadistically to reassure you that you're dispensable, in order to keep your attention?

Are you loyal? Will you lead me to the true center, or mislead me into folly? Will you fructify me or leave me alone and barren? How can I know your voice? Will I find you in the world, or only through renouncing the world? What, of me, are you? Where, in me, are you? Do you exist outside of the imaginative schemas of nineteenth-century men?

My confusion about you stems partly from the fact that your functions, as supposed by analytical psychology, sound mightily like "ego," as we have generally come to define it in heroic terms. Come to think of it, you sound quite a bit like "God," when It is Whom the patriarchal worlds describe as He. If you are Logos, whose voice speaks you? The voice of reason? The voice of conscience? The voice of the Holy Spirit? The voice of We, the People? The voice of one crying in the desert, "Prepare ye the way of the Lord"?[26] All of

---

[26] Isa. 40:3, Authorized (King James) Version.

the above? Does the heroine exist who is not under your spell? How can you connect me to my Deity, the One who is both male and female, creator and destroyer, now and forever, indivisible?

> O animus
> everywhere i see you
> ever-changing triptych of male beauty
> sensitive sensuals
> tall-walking and lithe
> On my red skateboard
> i zoom by you
>   in mukluks
>   sneakers
>   sandals
>   or shoeless
> You try and catch my hair
> you don't see my trajectory—
> skateboard aimed for outer space
>   thru inner space
>   thru you, Love,
>   and back again[27]

In trying to understand where the animus lives in the psyche of a woman, it may be helpful first of all to place it in relationship to ego. In Jung's schema, the ego consists of all we are conscious of being. That which we exclude is defined as shadow. Anima and animus are subsumed under the shadow in early life, and are gradually brought into conscious focus through experience and introspection. At first we cannot differentiate these structures of the psyche, nor can we tell which is functioning through our outward behavior.

A generation ago this sexist little rhyme didn't raise an eyebrow:

> What are little girls made of? What are little girls made of?
> Sugar and spice and everything nice, that's what little girls are
>   made of.
> What are little boys made of? What are little boys made of?
> Snakes and snails and puppy dog tails, that's what little boys are
>   made of.

---

[27] "O Animus," Claudia E. Lapp, *Cloud Gate,* p. 1.

Many children today would consider it strange. As one thoughtful child said to me, "It sounds very stereotypical." It is an extreme form of stereotyping, but subtle variations of this sort of thing continue to subliminally teach that "boys will be boys" and girls will not. By such conditioning girls and boys gradually form egos that accept certain characteristics as their own and eliminate others. At first what is deemed unacceptable is not only different, but bad. Only with experience do the qualities of the opposite sex which we find within become tolerable as something potentially valuable.

Animus is the archetypal masculine principle as it exists in a woman. When Jung conceived the term, the stereotyping of females and males into consistent gender roles and characteristics made the masculine principle as it exists in a woman easier to define than it is today. Jung assumed that the consciousness of a woman is identified by her biological sexual being; having the external genitalia of a female automatically meant having the ego of a female. Anima was who you were, and animus was who you eliminated from your self-definition. In that case, the experience of the unconscious would be perceived by the female in terms of otherness, and this otherness would be masculine.

The animus, an archetype unknowable in itself, manifests in three ways: through cultural expression, through biological influence, and through recurrent events in the history of the individual. While the biological influences on maleness and femaleness have not changed to any obvious degree since Jung's time, enormous cultural changes are occurring in the perception of the sexes.

Think about how our culture has presented the concept of what is "masculine" over the past hundred years. Many of our notions of masculine values remain unchanged. We admire strength of character and physical prowess in men. Yet many men today are not afraid of appearing vulnerable, of cultivating emotional intimacy in relationships with both men and women, of being present to birth and nurture children, of questioning traditional macho social forms, of grooming and dressing themselves in ways once reserved for women. Occupations formerly considered masculine—senior management, the judiciary, clergy and military, to name but a few—are no longer the prerogative of men.

Think about the great differences in the personal history of many women today, compared to women of a hundred years ago: exposure to many more men, and to different types of men; greater intimacy and communications with men; greater access to education and jobs; many more opportunities fostering independence; more support for self-assertion and creative expression.

Cultural changes in the past century have led to further differentiation of the issues surrounding sexual identity. It is now popularly held that biological sexual identity consists of factors beyond those that produce the external genitalia, that hormonal influences of both sexes exist in all humans, and that the external genitalia do not in every instance mirror the dominance of the sexual hormones. It is possible to be male or female genitally while having a range of contrasexual physiological characteristics (breast size, facial hair, voice timbre, muscular apportionment, etc.).

Complicating this is the fact that cultural conditioning has a strong influence on how biological males and females experience their masculinity and femininity. A hundred years ago the cultural factors were so strong that biological preferences were overridden by gender expectations. Choices that we have come to take for granted in the expression of gender roles were not possible. Jane Wheelwright, taught and analyzed by Jung, commented on this cultural change:

Women of the educated younger generations on the whole are independent, energetic, up-front, experimental. They handle their legitimate anger, assert their honest opinions and make necessary objections. In my day, a woman behaving in this way would have been condemned as an animus hound and indeed would have been acting and speaking out of society's collective animus. When caught by that collective pressure, i.e., when she expressed female potential that society had arbitrarily dumped into the animus category, woman would be forced to function from out of the animus complex, doing its bidding, instead of doing the bidding of her own biological ego. Her good qualities, when commandeered and distorted by the animus complex would have made her unrelated instead of independent; compulsive instead of energetic. She would have been devious, not upfront, fearful instead of experimental, hostile but not legitimately angry, opinionated rather than presenting her viewpoint. To put it bluntly she would have been objectionable instead of objecting. The primary business of the animus is to be a creative tool. Its secondary role is to give the necessary stamina to all endeavors. When the animus is overloaded with what does not belong to it, it takes on a negative stance, spilling over and destroying relationships. For this reason I feel knowledge of the animus is important today for women of all ages.[28]

Previously men strived to live up to society's expectation that they become husbands, fathers, aggressors, even though they might have no inclination or ability to do so. Women with no desire for motherhood were forced to live out their lives feeling like failures or withdrawing, usually in some noncreative way. There were courageous or accidental exceptions, but few people of either sex could find realistic models for nonconventional identities. There are always people with a seemingly innate talent for individuation who are able to go their own staunch way without obvious models or support, although on close examination there usually exists in their history a very strong, supportive parent who imbues a healthy spirit of conviction and high self-esteem. Such individuals live by their dreams and instincts without collective encouragement, and they forge new routes for all of us.

There were, therefore, women who not only survived but excelled in masculine fields of interest during Jung's day, even though they probably met with disapproval or animosity; and there were men who lived productive lives out of the anima. But on the whole, most men and women at least put forth the appearance of living up to the expectations set upon them by society, or they withdrew. This meant that Jung was accurate in observing that the unconscious personality of a woman was represented by the masculine principle, which combined all those qualities we associate with yang and Logos.

Today, many of those qualities—assertiveness, clarity of ideation, logical intellect, articulateness of mental processes, drive, etc.—are modeled for women by individuals of either sex. These psychological capacities include mental and emotional factors that were once ascribed to males exclusively, and when these ego-strengths became obvious in women, women often denied or hid them. Men, meanwhile, denied or hid their capacities for fantasy, receptivity, contem-

---

[28] *For Women Growing Older,* pp. 52-53.

plation and other qualities which in some circles were considered sissified, but which today we see as particular strengths of the yin ego, whether in man or woman.[29]

These cultural changes complicate the task of understanding what the female biological ego really is, and what the animus, as "other," is. Theoretically, the animus is a psychological function mediating between a woman's ego and the unconscious. In Jung's model of the psyche, the persona mediates between the ego and the outer world, while the contrasexual archetypes, anima and animus, are essentially guides to the inner world. On the journey of individuation, one must come to terms with the shadow before being able to relate in a conscious way to the anima and animus.

As archetypal feminine and masculine principles, anima and animus have a timeless place in every human psyche. The dominant archetype does not always match a person's biological sex. Anima values usually dominate the conscious psyche of a woman, but not in every woman, and not in every life situation. To illustrate the complexity of this, here is a description of three women, all in their twenties, who do not fit the usual picture.

Becky, a young woman from a large family, has had problems relating to her alcoholic mother all her life. Her father is a likable but ineffectual man. When Becky entered therapy she was depressed and anxious. She worked as a teacher and had just been through her first relationship with a man, which had ended in her being rejected.

Becky repeatedly dreamed of herself as a male, usually in the role of rescuing a female. The recurrence of the masculine dream ego suggested that Becky identified with men, and indeed, she had been a tomboy, had not dated at all until recently and had never had a satisfying sexual relationship. The recurrent theme of rescue suggested a repressed feminine side that called out for recognition.

She had not been in therapy for long when she met and fell in love with a young man. They were immediately compatible sexually and in every other way, and after a year of courtship they married and moved away. I do not have information about her dreams since then. I do know that after several years she was still happily married. Her

---

[29] See below, pp. 36ff.

identification on some level with men did not prevent Becky from making a conventional adjustment as a woman. She had not been in therapy long enough to assume that this was due to therapy. One can only surmise that when the conditions were favorable and she felt supported and safe, her feminine ego was accessible for a mature relationship.

Dana, in contrast, always a tomboy also, remembered having excited feelings about girls from the time she began school. She adamantly refused to wear dresses from an early age, and after a few years of high school dating which she found distasteful, declared herself a lesbian.

Dana's dreams in the early stage of therapy often presented her as a person harassed and persecuted by unsavory women. It seemed as if her conscious ego was male, so that even though her dream ego pictured her in a female body, she saw the "other" as women aggressors. The opposite sex, still fused with a persecutory shadow, was female. Dana's relationship with her mother appeared to be positive; however, her early life was fraught with chaotic changes through divorces, marriages, moves, and animosity between her several sets of parents.

Marie, like Becky, was one of many children of a domineering mother. She earned attention from her powerful and often absent father by excelling in sports. Although she was very attracted to men and boys as a young girl, she fell in love with a female celebrity and entered into a long-term relationship with her. Defining herself as lesbian, she was later surprised to find herself attracted to strong men and frequently propositioned by authority figures. She entered therapy, confused and anxious, after several relationships with men had come close to being consummated. She repeatedly dreamed about figures entering her bedroom, which frightened her and woke her before they could be identified. She found herself attracted to both men and women; she was afraid of being intimate with men, though in fantasy this excited her.

These examples, typical of issues raised by patients today, reflect changing roles and values, and changing images of the structure of the psyche. Psychology does not dictate normality, it studies the data presented by life. Today's women are vibrant though confused, open and questioning, unwilling to have answers foisted upon them.

It has been the special talent of women historically to follow and discriminate between the nuances and important details of relatedness. Forced into positions of waiting, of observing cyclical patterns of nature in their own physiological and emotional movements, and of remaining centered in the face of demands of children and men, women have had opportunities to observe these nuances for ages. Now they have more opportunities to express those observations.

Rachel Eliza Mann, for instance, a bright and creative graduate student in her twenties, struggles for integrity and awareness in her relationships with family, friends and romantic partners. The following poem explores aspects of dream figures and herself, including her masculine side. The kind of differentiation in fantasy represented here pays off in encounters in the outer world by preparing the ego for the tasks of sorting, unraveling, spinning and weaving that take place in the psyche during the course of a relationship.

> The lynx paces within its cage,
> The lunatic waits outside the door.
> Who is kept outside, who kept in?
> The second man makes love to one woman.
> Hands and lips wander like a meandering ant,
> an answering, a needing, a waiting.
>
> The first man's right hand opens up the door.
> So invited, the lunatic comes in.
> The lynx leaps, quivering and ready.
> She is opened up, the second man enters in.
> She dives alone into the Blue Hole,
> only her left hand keeping hold.
>
> The lynx dissolves into leaves.
> The lunatic crosses the river into the hall.
> The first man serves him porcupine stew.
> The second man plunges to her roots.
> The ant finds its queen.
> She takes hold and enters him.[30]

Confusion about what is animus and what is ego occurs because

---

[30] "Two Loves, an Ant, a Lynx, and a Lunatic" (unpublished).

ego-functions as defined by psychologists are subject to the bias of male dominance. I have come to use the terms "yin-ego" and "yang-ego" to emphasize the fact that because the ego has struggled to differentiate itself from the unconscious does not mean that all ego-functions must be heroic. In fact, such an ego would be maladaptive and self-destructive over time.

Energy itself cannot be identified as masculine. The uroboros may seem feminine to the male, but as the Great Spirit/Matter, it is androgynous, the organizing Self that drives the ego, as Dylan Thomas's "force that through the green fuse drives the flower."[31] To view the ego's creation from the unconscious as an image of birth from a mother, one would have to note that the creative phallus of the father was an essential aspect of the unconscious fruition, and that the fetus not only initiates but also passively receives the process. Ego is not, then, necessarily yang; it has feminine characteristics from the beginning. Though the yin-ego is by definition passive, passivity is not without energy. Yin qualities enable the ego to reflect, image, contain, generalize and empathize, and to embrace one's frailty.[32]

In the following poem Levertov describes a process of examining the inner landscape, probing its depths, its strengths and weaknesses, all part of the functions of a healthy ego.

> "I am a landscape," he said,
> "a landscape and a person walking in that landscape.
> There are daunting cliffs there,
> and plains glad in their way
> of brown monotony. But especially
> there are sinkholes, places
> of sudden terror, of small circumference
> and malevolent depths."
> "I know," she said. "When I set forth
> to walk in myself, as it might be
> on a fine afternoon, forgetting,
> sooner or later I come to where sedge

---

[31] Dylan Thomas, "The Force That Through the Green Fuse Drives the Flower," *Collected Poems,* p. 10.

[32] See below, pp. 61-62, for Fordham's list of ego functions.

and clumps of white flowers, rue perhaps,
mark the bogland, and I know
there are quagmires there that can pull you
down, and sink you in bubbling mud."
"We had an old dog," he told her, "when I was a boy,
a good dog, friendly. But there was an injured spot
on his head, if you happened
just to touch it he'd jump up yelping
and bite you. He bit a young child,
they had to take him down to the vet's and destroy him."
"No one knows where it is," she said,
"and even by accident no one touches it.
It's inside my landscape, and only I, making my way
preoccupied through my life, crossing my hills,
sleeping on green moss of my own woods,
I myself without warning touch it,
and leap up at myself—"
"—or flinch back
just in time."
        "Yes, we learn that.
It's not terror, it's pain we're talking about:
those places in us, like your dog's bruised head,
that are bruised forever, that time
never assuages, never."[33]

So entwined have the characteristics of animus and ego become
that many psychologists define ego strength entirely in terms of masculine adjectives. What women perceive as strength has at times been
considered weakness when judged by male values. Indeed, people of
both sexes have been hospitalized as severely disturbed for behavior
that could be judged as heroic from the standpoint of the yin ego. A
contemplative lifestyle, for instance, unless practiced under the aegis
of a religious institution, would be considered abnormal by some
psychologists' standards. A religious attitude in itself has been criticized as a form of weakness, a delusional system to avoid the pain of
mortality, according to those who define "normality" as extroverted
and rational. Yin ego-consciousness seems to be imaginal and synthesizing, and yang ego-consciousness factual and analytical.

---

[33] "Zeroing In," *Breathing the Water,* p. 19.

Good parenting requires much yin energy. Young children need waiting for, not hurrying; to have all their feelings held, not judged; to be contained, not driven. Yang-consciousness, oriented toward the future and efficiency, has difficulty here. I have found it easiest to catch my negative animus when I have been hurrying—then I have been most unkind and unconnected to my children. Our schools often reward only the yang ego, and the child who reflects yin experience is misplaced. A bright, introverted child of ten told me she found school going too quickly for her. "When the teacher says something that reminds me of something else, my mind wants to think of it; but if I do, then I find the rest of the class goes on to something else and I am lost." That is how the creative thought process becomes discouraged. Parents often judge themselves harshly for lacking patience. It is understandable, for yin-consciousness has been poorly modeled and unsupported, except in rare subcultures.

A brilliant woman told me she was considered retarded by her early teachers, not an unusual situation. Neglected, unkempt, the child of alcoholic parents, she was noticed, tested (IQ, 70), tolerated, but never touched until her second-grade teacher bothered to sit close to her and teach her to read with their fingers touching the book. This was all it took for the awakening to happen. Because that teacher shared a moment of grace with her, enabling her to feel received and not judged, her intellect was able to flourish.

> I have learned to fail. And I have had my say.
> Yet shall I sing until my voice crack (this being my leisure, this
>   my holiday)
> That man was a special thing and no commodity, a thing im-
>   proper to be sold.[34]

The confusion caused by the defining of ego in predominantly masculine terms has led some psychologists to wonder whether the term "ego" is useful at all, and whether the psyche can be conceived of as egoless, without a "monotheism of consciousness."[35]

---

[34] Edna St. Vincent Millay, from "Lines Written in Recapitulation," *Collected Poems,* p. 384.

[35] See James Hillman, *Anima: An Anatomy of a Personified Notion,* pp. 177-181.

My own practice is to think of ego as representing yin/yang features, because phenomenologically we are so accustomed to the experience of a central, organized aspect of the personality which can contain awareness of many parts, that it is difficult to imagine an egoless personality structure maneuvering its way between polarities.

> I would have joy,
> Hathor's joy and merriment and song,
> I would have it,
> Were it not for this
> Downward pull of darkness
> Drowning all in its wake.
>
> I would have peace,
> Jesus' peace that passes understanding,
> I would have it,
> Were it not for this
> Raging restlessness
> That rumbles and shakes.
>
> I would have love,
> Aphrodite's love, passionate and pleasuring,
> I would have it,
> Were it not for this
> Negative memory of men,
> Hades, Zeus, St. Paul, and even my kin.
>
> I would have wholeness,
> The Tao's seamless, balanced circle of wholeness,
> I would have it,
> Were it not for this
> Boundless ego without
> And this volcanic chaos within.[36]

Every woman contains within her psyche the masculine principle, though it may be very repressed. The better the relationship to the masculine principle, the more the woman is able to use animus qualities in appropriate ways throughout her life, and the less conflict she has about doing so. This means that in most women the masculine

---

[36] Glenda Taylor, "I Would Have It," *Life Is a River,* p. 36.

principle will be experienced as "other," but the relationship to that "other" may be quite positive.

When the principle of the opposite sex is dominant and unconscious, it obliterates the functioning of the ego and results in problems, especially in close relationships. But the more experience the ego has in dialogue with the contrasexual principle, the more ego-syntonic the relationship with the contrasexual partner becomes and the more choices one has in one's repertoire of conscious behavior. This is why male-female relationships in the outer world promote the blending of yin-yang qualities in the personalities of both men and women. Without the opportunity for positive outer experiences, one has to work harder to come to good terms with the inner partner.

It is still possible, however, to have a good relationship with the contrasexual archetype without much contact with outer-world partners, if one is aware of the capacity to use information from the unconscious to understand this powerful inner partner.

*

It has been said of Emily Dickinson that she, with Walt Whitman, "all but invented American poetry."[37] She was, in her "strange, explosive ponderings,"[38] prolific, but during her lifetime of reticence and obscurity, only eight of her 1800 poems were published. She said of her awesome father—a lawyer, congressman, treasurer of Amherst College—"His heart was pure and terrible, and I think no other like it exists."[39] She could not bear to attend his funeral; she listened to it alone in an upstairs bedroom. Her mother, kind, patient, pious and sickly, evoked condescension and even contempt from Emily, who hated the social duties of housekeeping and sewing imposed on women.

Dickinson left home at seventeen to attend Mt. Holyoke, a few miles away, but returned home, never to leave, before the year was up.

---

[37] Ellman and O'Clair, *Norton Anthology,* p. 33.
[38] Ibid.
[39] Ibid., p. 34.

We know of two men with whom Emily Dickenson corresponded, but, like her sister, she never married. Some cataclysm occurred in her inner life around 1861, an event only indirectly referred to in her poetry but probably having to do with an experience of unrequited love. From that time on, her poetry changed. She seemed to have been transformed from girl to woman. In spite of a seemingly uneventful life on the surface, she left a treasure of inner riches. Her authenticity and self-sufficiency are reflected in this self-image:

The Soul selects her own Society—
Then—shuts the Door—
To her divine Majority—
Present no more—

Unmoved—she notes the Chariots—pausing—
At her low Gate—
Unmoved—an Emperor be kneeling
Upon her Mat—

I've known her—from an ample nation—
Choose One—
Then—close the Valves of her attention—
Like Stone—[40]

Though she rarely left the house, she could find the metaphysical world reflected in her small environment, as expressed in "There's a certain Slant of light."[41] And though she ostensibly experienced little intimacy, she wrote this now famous line: "Parting is all we know of heaven. And all we need of hell."[42] As Bennett notes:

She was a woman who had come to terms with herself, with both her strengths and her losses, and who knew how to balance one against the other in order to be faithful to the "Mystery" she served within.[43]

Lad of Athens, faithful be
To Thyself,

---

[40] *The Poems of Emily Dickinson,* no. 303.
[41] Ibid., no. 258.
[42] Ibid., no. 1732.
[43] *My Life a Loaded Gun,* p. 93.

And Mystery—
All the rest is Perjury—[44]

The absence of the opposite sex in a person's early life does not mean that there is an absence of the archetypal energy associated with the "other"; but without a human relationship to mitigate the powerful energies of the contrasexual archetype, its effects are especially strong. The opposite sex is likely to be idealized or feared, to be treated more as a god or goddess than as an ordinary person. Similarly, when members of the opposite sex are one-sided in a child's eyes—when father or mother is very, very good, or very, very bad—their opposite is likely to fill the vacuum. Hence we have the kinds of attractions between opposites, and especially opposites in terms of social status, that are so common in adolescence.

This phenomenon is more complicated than this explanation implies, but the failure of the parent to present a three-dimensional person to the child is an important factor. The Self will try to fill in with a needed experience of reality testing, and this must be understood by parents, especially in today's world of single-parent and step-parented homes.

Obviously, the pressure on a parent to provide safe limits and security while still accepting his or her own shadow-side in the child's imagery poses quite a difficult task. The ability to do this presupposes considerable development on the part of the parent; few of us have this ability when we begin parenting. Disclosing our own vulnerabilities while modeling firm values and expectations is not simple. It is what we aspire to. But children also need something to aspire to, something to hope for.

Glenda Taylor describes the power of the missing parent:

You had no right to die
and leave me here alone, fatherless.

I was only two years old.
I needed you. Why didn't you know?

Never mind that others called you
useless, unreliable, drunk, a hollow gourd.

---

[44] *The Poems of Emily Dickinson,* no. 1768.

I never listened.
Dead, you were my childhood's knight, my god,
a fantasy, larger than life, other than flesh,
a perfect, primary male archetype,
imprinted on air.

Your dying made it hard.
What other—stepfather, let us say,
or later, what young man—
could measure up to one
who never had to prove, in daily doses,
his godhood?

What years it took and work to reach the place
where now, at last, mature, I mourn the human you
I never knew—broken, scarred, sad—
no shining armor to be sure, yet a man
I might have known
simply as
my Dad.[45]

And Millay writes about the anguish of missing the experience of the "other," in "The Princess Recalls Her One Adventure":

Hard is my pillow
Of down from the duck's breast,
Harsh the linen cover;
I cannot rest.

Fall down, my tears,
Upon the fine hem,
Upon the lonely letters
Of my long name;
Drown the sigh of them.

We stood by the lake
And we neither kissed nor spoke;
We heard how the small waves
Lurched and broke,
And chuckled in the rock.

---

[45] "Absent Father," in *Life Is a River,* p. 8.

We spoke and turned away.
We never kissed at all.
Fall down, my tears.
I wish that you might fall
On the road by the lake,
Where my cob went lame,
And I stood with the groom
Till the carriage came.[46]

With the inner partner, as in any relationship, there are good and bad times. Those who have done a lot of inner work are often surprised and disappointed when robbers or rapists appear in their dreams. They wonder why they should be vulnerable to such negative images. But self-understanding cannot protect us from all dangers; the dark side of the Self is ever present. Self-awareness helps us to recognize this part of ourselves and others, and not to deny it.

Disturbing dream encounters can be touched off by many factors—the invasion of a virus, the chance meeting with a sociopath or the shadow side of a spouse or close friend, an insight into a cultural trend—powerful events which can temporarily overwhelm the ego. No woman is so well integrated that she is not occasionally beset with the appearance of a negative animus figure. But usually, when the relationship to the animus is comfortable, the bad times are not nightmarish, only unfamiliar or uncomfortable.

It is one thing to talk about these concepts, quite another to identify them in real life situations. For a woman to recognize when she is possessed by the animus—that is, when her ego functioning has been displaced by the masculine archetype and she is under his spell—requires considerable introspection. Knowing when we have the help of the animus to implement our authentic task, as opposed to being under his thumb, is not easy.

I have always enjoyed writing poems, songs and letters. It came naturally early, and comforted me if I was lonely or bored. As such, it feels like a deeply feminine experience that is its own reward. I consider my professional writing animus driven. It requires an audience and must fulfill certain standards imposed by others. I think of

---

[46] *Collected Poems,* pp. 318-319.

ego as a good student-secretary-agent-director. Inspired by animus, she is spirited, analytical, abstract; inspired by anima, he is imaginal, synthesizing, personal.

Many fairy tales illustrate animus possession in terms of a woman imprisoned in a tower. This can be seen as a symbol of the feminine principle being out of touch with the earth, instinct. Such tales reflect a situation where a woman is too "high," through inflation, overintellectualization, unbalanced intuition or some other state of being ungrounded. The woman is considered to be overridden by animus attitudes, not because she has so much mental energy, but because that energy is not balanced by a connection with nature. This condition can be found in men as well as women. In men it would be considered an anima problem.

One way of recognizing animus possession is by observing that one feels driven or paralyzed, entranced or desperate.[47] The solution in fairy tales usually comes through some symbol of the woman's connection to nature and her ability to relate in an embodied way—helpful animals, a talisman given by a loving figure, her long tresses or a beautiful voice, etc.—or help comes in the form of a healthy, earthy male. In other words, by valuing a connection with nature her masculine sky-consciousness is balanced by embodied energy. To stay imprisoned means to forego attention to one's natural instincts.

Joan, for instance, worked so hard and with such focused attention that she never relaxed. At night she brought work home or cleaned her spotless house. Her husband was too frightened of being alone to confront her or insist on more attention. This is being in the tower. Joan was imprisoned by her slavery to an image of her father's abusive demands that she work hard all the time; he never allowed his children to take a day off. Saturdays were for housework, Sundays for church and cooking, schoolnights for study.

Joan easily worked herself into a prominent position in a profession dominated by men. She ignored nature in the form of fatigue and need for play, and ended up in the hospital every few weeks with severe headaches.

---

[47] Hillman points out that it is when we feel most sure of ourselves that we are caught in the grip of the collective contrasexual archetype and actually "most estranged from ourselves." (*Anima,* p. 83, quoting Jung)

Listening to her headaches was finally the way Joan responded to nature's call to get out of her head. A helpful part of herself, which we pictured as a kinder, more balanced aspect, could stand up to the powerful father memories and overcome their influence. One might say that this was ego, but the fact is her ego could not accomplish this before it gained some strength and assertiveness as a result of her inner work. This might be called animus-energy, culled out and differentiated from father-energy. It enabled her to make the effort to help herself, not to stay compulsively in a father-pleasing mode.

It is because of this task, the need to stay in balance with their feminine nature, that women keep journals, record dreams and ask for communication from their dream figures, lovers and friends, and especially from their own bodies. Feedback on animus issues is hard to come by. Many men shrink from the kind of intimate discussion which can bring clarity to the influence of the contrasexual partners in a relationship. Unfortunately, women often have to work alone on this differentiation of ego and animus.

4

Relationship with the Divine

Women have only recently begun to articulate the profound effect
that the absence of the feminine in Judeo-Christian images of God
has had on their images of themselves. How do we come to value
ourselves as much as the other when the other is male and God is
male? Who is animus, and who God? What happens to the little girl
presented with pictures of God which are exclusively masculine? By
the time her mind develops to the point where she can imagine God
as unknowable, beyond any anthropomorphizing images, the andro-
centric "reality" of the collective is already established.

How do we separate our human male partners, outer and inner,
from God? Even though we may see sexual or gender attributes of
the absolute God to be mere products of fallacious finite thinking—
the Supreme Being being unknowable and beyond duality—it is not
easy to fend off a lifetime of associating God with the pronoun "He."
It is easy to form the scarcely conscious conclusion that what we
come out of and return to in death, "the Earth Mother," is inferior to
what we strive to please and propitiate, "the Heavenly Father."

The reverence paid to the Madonna by Christian religions does not
fill the gap. The image of the Virgin, set before women as indicative
of our place in the scheme of things, was not without value. For a
long time, for many, it was a comfortable place in the orderly patriarchal cosmology, full of dignity, meaning and relatedness. Such a
view of womankind not only called forth great feminine strength, it
relieved us of many of the distractions that clutter our self-concept in
our current adaptation as man's equal. It also left more energy to de-
vote to homemaking and childcare. But we all know the high price
that was paid for that adaptation. The price for giving it up must also
be paid, until the full value of the feminine is integrated into collective consciousness.

The spirit of confusion and skepticism that our unbalanced images
of God have left us with is amusingly clear in Phyllis McGinley's
"The Day After Sunday":

47

> Always on Monday, God's name is in the morning papers,
>   His name is a headline, His Works are rumored abroad.
> Having been praised by men who are movers and shakers,
>   From prominent Sunday pulpits, newsworthy is God.
>
> On page 27, just opposite Fashion Trends,
>   One reads at a glance how He scolded the Baptists a little,
> Was firm with the Catholics, practical with the Friends,
>   To Unitarians pleasantly noncommittal.
> In print are His numerous aspects, too; God smiling,
>   God vexed, God thunderous, God whose mansions are pearl,
> Political God, God frugal, God reconciling
>   Himself with science, God guiding the Camp Fire Girl.
>
> Always on Monday morning the press reports
>   God as revealed to His vicars in various guises—
> Benevolent, stormy, patient, or out of sorts.
>   God knows which God is the God God recognizes.[48]

It is a tribute to the validity of the individuation process that many women were able to experience their self-worth, to value their intuition and instincts, and to prevail in the hope for equality as human beings under the cultural conditioning of centuries. The feminine Self, even without respected images in the collective consciousness, shone through the obscurity of prejudice and continues to prod us toward wholeness.

But it is also clear that the return of the Goddess is not a peaceful process, nor is the endpoint of the emergence of the fully acknowledged feminine emanation of the Divine yet within our view. The patriarchal God-image has damaged the wholeness of men as well as women, but in a very insidious way. It has generally enhanced the ego-inflated self-esteem of men while damaging their capacity for empathy, while in women it has contributed to low self-esteem and diminished their capacity to find their own authority. At least now it is possible for women to question the voices of authority, and not to assume they are all from God.

Equality—that is, mutual respect, with its need for endless nego-

---

[48] In Cleanth Brooks and Robert Penn Warren, eds., *Understanding Poetry,* pp. 339-340.

tiation, compromise and democratic process—is more cumbersome than the efficiency of totalitarianism. There are situations where survival depends on the delegation of authority to a leader. This line of reasoning, in itself nonobjectionable, has seduced women into giving up their own leadership potential. Women have begun to understand how they have delegated authority, often giving in too easily to the animus figures within, listening unquestioningly to constricting inner messages and, in outer life, not protesting against being degraded. With the ego identified as masculine, there was no feminine voice to raise a question.

It is no wonder that women have had to struggle and rebel in order to believe in their deepest truths, and that they have hidden so much of their wisdom over the centuries, even from themselves. Now that the images of the Great Goddesses have been recovered, women have found themselves drawn to an ancient aspect of themselves that has been joyously retrieved. The great hunger in women for Self images, feminine rituals and affirmation of the soul in feminine terms is now recognized. Women are magnetized, enlivened and inspired by these developments. This is apparent to those of us who are privileged to share in the intimate inner life of men and women through the fantasies and dreams they bring into analysis. The Goddess, returning from repression, now shows herself in dreams and poetry, sometimes with violent force. Often her first appearance in consciousness is as a dark woman.

I first encountered the Black Madonna in Switzerland, where Her presence made such a profound impression that I made several journeys to visit Her other shrines. She is known all over Europe, but especially in Poland and Czechoslovakia. There are different legends which attempt to explain on the mundane level how the statue of the Virgin Mary came to be black. Usually they involve the miraculous transformation of the statue during some violent invasion by heathen hordes. For me, in 1973, such explanations were irrelevant; it was the immediate emotional response to this symbol of the dark Goddess that gripped me and touched something ancient and compelling inside, as archetypal images do. It was love at first sight, marking a transformation in my relationship to the Divine. I wrote:

Black Mary, Black Mary, come down, come down!

In my cave I await you to speak in whispers
to sing, to sing in smiling secrets
for we were born on the ebb tide.

Black Mary, mother, you understand
the journey in darkness, the black mist, crevice
the damp and deep pulsating caverns
of those whose visions give birth to flame—
of those whose heat gives birth to vision . . .
beneath the day, beyond the light
in the southmost furnace of his red-rays lingered
and with what strength you bore the thrill,
the throbbing power of his hot sword's piercing;
oh what bull's might within you kept you
whole, while soaring through that frenzy,
catapulted through night's spaces!
Nuit, nuit, all is nuit
to those who choose the waning moon
to leap on in the spring to life—
Black Mary, I saw you, I saw you! You were
dancing close with the Midnite Sun,
you kissed in the sea, the night tides high
You didn't even care who saw you
knowing the warmth of the southwind's calling;
I saw you reach for his full power
you took his All into your Nothing.

And when he found your velvet blackness lovely
we cried for joy; then burned my candle brighter.

The work of historians, archaeologists, mythologists, theologians and psychologists, in piecing together the ancient world of the Goddess, is transforming the relationship to the Divine in the collective consciousness. The excavations of Neolithic villages in Europe have established the existence of a matriarchal social order which venerated the Goddess-Mother-Creator and the whole universe as extension and partaker of her divinity. In a foreword to Marija Gimbutas' archaeological work, Joseph Campbell describes this era as

an actual age of harmony and peace in accord with the creative energies of nature which for a spell of some 4000 prehistoric years anteceded the 5000 of what James Joyce has termed the "nightmare" (of contending tribal and national interests) from which it is now certainly time for this planet to wake.[49]

Gimbutas shows that the Old European culture, a peaceful, sedentary, agricultural world, valued art and life, looked at white as the color of death (bone) and black as the color of fertility. That culture was displaced by invasions of Indo-European nomads, horse-riding warriors who valued women as brides and adornments rather than creatrices, whose art was expressed primarily in weaponry, and who favored white and yellow as sky and sun colors. Gimbutas avers that we are still living under the sway of an aggressive male invasion and only beginning to discover our long alienation from our earth-centered heritage.

Jung contended that the Self archetype manifests in each individual as a drive toward wholeness, and that symbols of the Self often carry God-images into conscious life. Jung repeatedly explained that the tendency to find symbols of wholeness was inherent in human nature; he was not, he claimed, making statements about God, or about what human beings should do, he only pointed out what they *did* do. Since this was seen by him to be a universal factor in the psyche of humankind, Jung argued that it was within the aegis of psychology to deal with spiritual needs and the projection of God-images onto the Self.

Critics of Jung accuse him of overstepping the boundary between psychology and theology, and some go so far as to accuse him of founding a religion. This is in response to his concept of the archetypes, which Jung adopted from philosophers before him, especially Kant and Schiller. The archetype of the Self particularly causes disagreement because its relationship to God remains inexplicable, and its relationship to God-images confuses many people. Jung saw the Self, the unifying principle, as the carrier of the *experience* of God; this is not to reduce God to an experience. The prominence of this issue among both theologians and feminists interested in Jung's ideas warrants lengthier discussion than is possible here.[50]

---

[49] *The Language of the Goddess,* pp. xiii-xiv.
[50] Readers interested in pursuing this subject might start with the correspondence between Jung and Father Victor White, in *C.G. Jung Letters.*

My concern here is with how our culture has reflected the notion of male superiority by projecting the image of masculinity onto the Divine, and onto the Self as representative of the Divine in humankind. Even many therapists are prejudiced toward male Self images and do not recognize images of the Goddess when She appears in unconscious material. If the images of the Self reveal our model of integration, our model of wholeness, what does a strong sense of the feminine Self look like? Images of the Self-supported personality are often colored by masculine qualities; we picture independence, detachment, self-sufficiency. But there is also an embodied, related, caring Self. The individuated personality is not without tension, not without distress, not necessarily unflappable. On the contrary, emotions have as much value in the totality of being as tranquility.

Archetypal energies deriving from the Self keep us moving, not transfixed. Tensions may bring outrage, grief and love. No evolved human being can be separate from human relatedness for long. When ego needs are resolved, as they often are in later life, the need to give to others propels us onward, into transactions both serene and calamitous. The support of the Self gives us the freedom to move from relatedness to solitary reflection and back to relatedness, in a continual flow of soul and spirit.

Jung's psychology recognizes that there is a larger influence on our lives than the conscious mind can possibly take in. It recognizes an innate need to find some relationship to the Divine in order to give meaning to life. This does not make analysis a religion. Analysis is an attempt to understand our own nature; it tells us nothing about the nature of God, which remains a mystery. It may help us to become more responsive to the signs of God. One of the results of successful therapy of any kind is that a person becomes self-actualizing. Many therapists have observed that the self-actualized person is better able to integrate spirituality into day-to-day life.

The flow of feminine and masculine energies makes it possible for us to project both authority and mercy onto our God-images. This integration is not easily achieved because of the masculine/feminine split in Western religion. That split is seen in the incapacity to fall into God, or to rest on the breasts of God, as the mystics do. Here is Teresa of Avila:

O Lord of my life.
Sustenance that sustains me.

From those divine breasts
where it seems God is always
sustaining the soul
there flow streams of milk
bringing comfort
to all the people of the castle.

It seems the Lord desires
that in some manner
these others in the castle
may enjoy the great gift
the soul is enjoying.

From that full-flowing river,
where this tiny fount is swallowed up,
a spurt of that water
will sometimes be directed
toward the sustenance of those
who in corporal things
must serve these two who are wed.[51]

This capacity for trust is inherent in the positive feminine Self image. Jung spoke of the archetype of the coniunctio, the sacred marriage, that moves us to seek the union of opposites, just as we once struggled to separate the amorphous whole. One of the most universal experiences of that energy is being in love, our metaphor on the human plane for the connection with the Source on a metaphysical level.

I have had people tell me they do not know the experience of awe, and often the same persons will not fall in love because they don't want to lose themselves. I am speaking here of a conviction, not of a temporary decision to postpone romantic union for the sake of a more pressing priority. This refusal to surrender tells me that the connection to the feminine Self is tenuous. Falling in love can be denigrated as adolescent or weak only when the feminine is devalued. At any age, to fall in love is to trust that one will survive the

---

[51] "Breasts of God," *Meditations with Teresa of Avila,* p. 120.

possible loss of the loved one. Rather than fearing the loss of Self, one must have the utmost faith in Self to risk the depths of intimacy while maintaining balance and integrity. Rather than diminishing Self, falling in love reveals new aspects of the Self that have been projected onto the beloved. This is why it is so enriching, even when unrequited and unconsummated.

Accustomed as we are to see falling in love as Eros-given, a passive wounding by cupid's arrow, we may ignore the presence of Aphrodite behind the scene—Aphrodite, goddess of transformation, also known as Ishtar or Isis. The transforming goddesses correspond to the masculine gods, such as Hermes and Osiris, who bring the fullness of spirit to accompany the soul-deepening effects of the conjoining. Love, as transformation, is not just sweetness. It wrenches and twists in its transformative role.

Images of the feminine Self manifest in terms of relatedness and caring, but this movement of the feminine evokes a reciprocal movement of the masculine. Mary, the God-lover and God-mother; Isis, the God-lover, God-sister, God-wife and God-mother; Tara, the feminine emanation of the compassionate Buddha who chooses to be a comforter of all sentient beings rather than remain in Nirvana; Sophia, partner of God, personifying compassion and wisdom—all reverberate with the responsive, fructifying phallic power. Though it is possible to receive affirmation from male God-images, it is a strong connection with the feminine Self that sustains women. Once, during a stressful time, I dreamed of being nourished through an umbilical cord attached to the sap of a huge tree. I saw this as an extremely deep and primitive connection to the Nature Goddess. Called or not called, the Goddess is present, preserving and restoring, keeping us rooted.

Robert Graves has upheld the belief that poetry has always been one of the manifestations of the Goddess. In *The White Goddess,* he amplifies his thesis with evidence from ancient bards of the sacred aspects of the poetic muse. Perhaps it is this emanation of Goddess-energy that makes poetry such an attractive medium for the exploration of the masculine at this point in collective consciousness.

Throughout women's poetry, the clear loyalty to nature reveals a connection to the feminine side of God. For example, simple faith, the capacity to rest on the divine breasts, is shown here by Elizabeth Bishop:

> Think of the storm roaming the sky uneasily
> like a dog looking for a place to sleep in,
> listen to its growling.
>
> Think how they must look now, the mangrove keys
> lying out there unresponsive to the lightning
> in dark, coarse-fibered families,
>
> where occasionally a heron may undo his head,
> shake up his feathers, make an uncertain comment
> when the surrounding water shines.
>
> Think of the boulevard and the little palm trees
> all stuck in rows, suddenly revealed
> as fistfuls of limp fish-skeletons.
>
> It is raining there. The boulevard
> and its broken sidewalks with weeds in every crack,
> are relieved to be wet, the sea to be freshened.
>
> Now the storm goes away again in a series
> of small, badly-lit battle scenes,
> each in "Another part of the field."
>
> Think of someone sleeping in the bottom of a row-boat
> tied to a mangrove root or the pile of a bridge;
> think of him as uninjured, barely disturbed.[52]

The danger of assuming a God who ascends too far above the natural world (and leaves the Goddess of love unattended!) is reflected upon by Mona Van Duyn:

> *Amazing research proves simple prayer makes flowers grow*
> *many times faster, stronger, larger.—Advertisement in The*
> *Flower Grower.*
>
> I pray that the great world's flowering stay as it is,
> that larkspur and snapdragon keep to their ordinary size,
> and bleedingheart hang in its old way, and Judas tree

---

[52] "Little Exercise," in Brooks and Warren, *Understanding Poetry,* pp. 370-371.

stand well below oak, and old oaks color the fall sky.
For the myrtle to keep underfoot, and no rose
to send up a swollen face, I pray simply.

There is no disorder but the heart's. But if love goes leaking
outward, if shrubs take up its monstrous stalking,
all greenery is spurred, the snapping lips are overgrown,
and over oaks red hearts hang like the sun.
Deliver us from its giant gardening, from walking
all over the earth with no rest from its disproportion.

Let all flowers turn to stone before ever they begin to share
love's spaciousness, and faster, stronger, larger
grow from a sweet thought, before any daisy
turns, under love's gibberellic wish, to the day's eye.
Let all blooms take shape from cold laws, down from a cold air
let come their small grace or measurable majesty.

For in every place but love the imagination lies
in its limits. Even poems draw back from images
of that one country, on top of whose lunatic stemming
whoever finds himself there must sway and cling
until the high cold God takes pity, and it all dies
down, down into the great world's flowering.[53]

May Sarton's "The Invocation to Kali" is a poem in honor of the
dark Goddess. In it she recognizes the power of Kali as the dark side
of our natures and of nature herself, who must be given Her due.
Here is part of the second section, "The Kingdom of Kali":

Every creation is born out of the dark.
Every birth is bloody. Something gets torn.
Kali is there to do her sovereign work
Or else the living child will be stillborn.

She cannot be cast out (she is here for good)
Nor battled to the end. Who wins that war?
She cannot be forgotten, jailed, or killed.
Heaven must still be balanced against her.

---

[53] "The Gardener to His God," ibid., pp. 456-457.

Out of destruction she comes to wrest
The juice from the cactus, its harsh spine,
And until she, the destroyer, has been blest,
There will be no child, no flower, and no vine.[54]

Moral evolutionists, maintaining that dense is base and rarified is better, urge us to transcendence. As I see it, life on earth gives us the responsibility to stay grounded and to consider the possibility that aggression and compassion have one source. No matter how evolved we may feel our consciousness to be, there is always shadow.

Finally, let us consider Emily Dickinson's commitment to an earth-oriented divinity:

This is my letter to the World
That never wrote to Me—
The simple News that Nature told—
With tender Majesty
Her Message is committed
To Hands I cannot see—
For love of Her— Sweet— countrymen—
Judge tenderly— of Me.[55]

[54] *Collected Poems,* pp. 316-317.
[55] *The Poems of Emily Dickinson,* no. 441.

5
Animus Development

When a man controls his anima, or a woman her animus, they are doing something no one dreamed of doing before; because mankind has always been possessed. When you dare to free yourself, you get into a new order of things, and that means a challenge to the old order . . . .

If a man makes a modest attempt at controlling his anima, he will at once be forced into a situation where he is tested to the limit . . . and it is the same with a woman: every devil around will do his best to get at her animus . . . it is as if a vacuum has been created and everything rushes in to fill it. That is why people who attempt to control these figures get into new situations that almost force them back to their former state; it works quite automatically.

For one should realize that one risks an unusual loneliness in controlling the animus or the anima. This is because a *participation mystique* is created by not controlling them; when one allows a piece of one's self to wander about and be projected into other people, it gives one a feeling of being connected. And most connections in the world are of this sort. *Participation mystique* provides this appearance of a connection, but it is never a real connection, it is never a relationship; it only gives one the feeling of being a sheep in the flock. And that is, of course, something; for if you disqualify yourself as a sheep, then you are necessarily out of the flock, and you have to suffer a certain loneliness. Yet then you have a chance to reestablish a connection, and this time it can be a conscious relationship which is far more satisfactory.

—C.G. Jung, *The Visions Seminars.*

The habit of charting development is the prerogative and penchant of psychologists, who rely on systems, statistical norms and comparative techniques to create a language and an order for their observations. Without such ordering processes there is only the chaos of random observation and "common sense."

Developmental theory is a valid approach when seeking abstract knowledge of humankind, but it is risky to generalize or to judge persons according to where they are or should be on some linear scale. Any particular person may develop certain characteristics prior to or later than statistical expectations. Carefully examining the process of an individual personality, we see aspects of the future as well as vestiges of the past, resulting in rich, fascinating differences.

Analysts seldom find it fruitful to evaluate patients in terms of developmental levels or norms of behavior, including psychiatric diagnoses, for this tends to impose an inhibiting structure on the analytic work. The goal of analysis is to explore the embodied psyche, to touch the untouched and believed-untouchable parts of the psyche without judgment or bias, and to allow the patient to follow the energy of the individuation process.

For example, it was not uncommon until recently to hear a critical judgment of women who never married. The word "spinster" carried an aura of lacking something. On closer examination we might find quite the opposite—complex personality resources, extremely refined sensibilities, a powerful capacity for dedication or sacrifices made consciously and with great integrity. Only after thorough understanding of a woman's experiences, choices, values and inner world, her dreams and creative expressions, can we begin to see whether she lacks something, and even then we are evaluating on the assumption that her lifetime on earth is all there is.

To name only two, the writers Flannery O'Connor and Emily Dickinson not only never married, but never ventured far from their parents' home for long; yet one could not judge either of these creative women as undeveloped. The many-splendored imagination of each implies more experience than some world travelers acquire. If we were to judge by the events in their lives, we might come to the false conclusion that their development was somehow impoverished. Such is the effect of overvaluing the exterior life, a common failing of an extroverted culture.

Nowadays there is a collective bias against the woman who chooses to be a homemaker and/or mother rather than have a career outside the home. These traditional roles have been so devalued by men and women who are possessed by the achievement-oriented masculine attitude that they are misperceived as simple and unchal-

lenging. Although child care can be coped with from a purely unconscious position, it takes supreme skill to care for children well and
creatively. Also, keeping oneself out of the marketplace and in the
home, where artistic and contemplative energies may flourish, seems
to me to merit applause, not shame. But again, extroverted collective
values may claim otherwise.

With the drawbacks of developmental schemes clearly in mind, let
us now proceed to look at some.

There are many ways of approaching developmental stages; the
fields of psychology, medicine and theology have produced an array
of them. Some of the best known are those of Jean Piaget, Abraham
Maslow, Arnold Gesell, Eric Erickson, Sigmund Freud, Melanie
Klein and Lawrence Kohlberg. Little differentiation by sex has characterized these theories, except that of Gesell, who observed significant differences in tested behavior of boys and girls of eighteen
months of age. Some have been thought to be insensitive to the process in females. For example, Freudian developmental theory, with
its focus on the oedipal stage, has been criticized for describing feminine development negatively, that is, in terms of the absence of valued attributes ascribed to males.[56] Kohlberg's theory of moral development has been criticized by feminists because it does not recognize a difference between the way women and men approach the
thinking through of moral questions. As Carol Gilligan has pointed
out, in *In a Different Voice,* women evaluate moral issues in a context of relationships and not as abstract questions of logic.

Except for important differences in emphasis on various factors,
such as sexual libido and genetics, Jung accepted Freud's description
of developmental stages. Jung focused on the influence of the mother
rather than the oedipal conflict, and he spoke of a pre-oedipal libido
which could not be identified as specifically sexual. He also identified the tendency of the psyche to split between the innate need to
develop and the unconscious pull to regress to earlier stages for
strengthening.

Two prominent Jungians in the area of developmental theory are
Eric Neumann and Michael Fordham. Their approaches are consider-

---

[56] Freudian theory continues to evolve. See below, pp. 63-64.

ably different. Neumann used mythology as his metaphor while Fordham arrived at his theories through years of observing infant behavior.

Fordham's work illuminates Jung's emphasis on genetic factors and differing archetypal influences on a person from the beginning of life. Fordham has found newborns to be far from formless and passive; he sees them as coming into the world with sophisticated skills for interacting with the environment. Their interactions are unique and call forth responses from the mothering person which vary from personality to personality. Each infant/mother pair is unique. We can't assume that siblings have the same experience of "mother," for each child pulls different energies into its life.

Fordham identifies the following usual ego-functions: perception, memory, organization of mental functioning, control over mobility, reality testing, speech, defenses (seen as necessary for self-preservation and not necessarily pathological), and the capacity to relinquish control.[57]

In *The Origins and History of Consciousness,* Neumann describes developmental stages of consciousness not only in individual lives but also in the history of humankind, as reflected in mythology and culture. But he recognized that a male-oriented culture could not adequately envision feminine development. Even though the movement of the ego toward the union of opposites—the final stage of transformation, which Jung called the coniunctio—applied to both men and women, Neumann went on to describe stages in the development of women which contained some unique turns, especially in relationship to the mother.

The first stage, psychic unity, is the same for both sexes. This is the prototype for every situation of unconscious identity, which Jung called *participation mystique.*

In Neumann's view, the psyche, whose center is the Self, initially exists in a state of "immediate identity" with the body, so that the Self bears the attributes of the exterior physical sex, whose hormonal condition is closely connected with psychological processes.[58] The

---

[57] *Children As Individuals,* pp. 93-96. These views are discussed in Andrew Samuels, *Jung and the Post-Jungians,* pp. 55-88.

[58] It was noted here in chapter two that this assumption can be challenged.

male, then, experiences identification with the mother, the feminine other, as a relationship with the non-Self and must achieve a certain detachment and an objective attitude toward this primary relationship in order to preserve his masculine identification.

According to Neumann, a girl's original identity with mother can last throughout life without interfering with her experience of herself as feminine. He held that women's first and natural way of relating is by identification, because the experience with mother has not had to be severed, and that longing for this kind of relatedness accompanies women throughout life and is especially fulfilled in pregnancy.

Neumann called the second stage, arrived at when the feminine ego recognizes its separateness from the unconscious, the Self-conserving stage. Here the focus is on being safe within familiar feminine perimeters. The woman relates to other women and children, whereas men are experienced as alien and strangers whom she will fear or else manipulate as objects.

The third stage is invasion by the Paternal Uroboros, envisioned as a seizure of the woman's consciousness by a transforming, numinous power, which he imagined as feeling like being taken by a male divinity. Through surrender to this power the feminine ego submits to a transformation which pulls her away from her attachment to the exclusively feminine world, but keeps her enthralled to the masculine in a submissive posture.

In the fourth stage, the Patriarchal Partner, there is some movement either from the inner masculine or through an outer man, freeing her from the father's grasp. This is not satisfactory in the long term, however, because the woman is still subservient to the male. While this may be appropriate on a social level, the suppression of her feminine esteem is the basis for conflict and illness.

True Confrontation, the fifth stage, occurs when the woman can meet others, including men, as whole persons, and can sacrifice convention for self-development. There is a recognition of the transpersonal in relationships and an acknowledgment of projection.

The sixth stage, Experience of the Female Self, brings integration, inner renewal, fruitfulness of mind and soul that is uniquely feminine. Self and ego are united, the true coniunctio.

Neumann gives no age range for any of these stages. He recognized that there are great differences in women (and men too) with regard to conscious development.

Emma Jung observed four stages of animus development, with appropriate personifications when they are projected onto men, in terms of physical power, initiative, intellectual power and finally spiritual power. Although I have not found this schema particularly useful clinically, it has generated interest. [59]

In a liberating examination of sociocultural, symbolic and personal dimensions of women's experience of themselves, Polly Young-Eisendrath and Florence Wiedemann use the psychologies of Jung and Jane Loevinger as major theoretical frameworks.[60] Sensitive to the conflicts inherent in female identity in our society, the authors avoided models of development which relied on "deficit thinking" to describe women. An example of thinking in terms of deficits is the medical model, which focuses on pathology and sees a person as the passive victim of circumstances; one has been attacked by an illness or is insufficient in some way. Recovery is placed in the hands of an authority.

Originally the Freudian model was a deficit model for women, as it assumed penis envy to be the key to female psychological development. The emphasis on caring and relatedness that is so important a part of women's psychological make-up was reduced to masochism. Little or no consideration of sociological factors mitigated Freud's reductive interpretation of feminine psychology. The fact that girls observed their mothers in the role of servants to a patriarchal God, society and husband, was not credited with contributing to their lack of self-esteem and autonomy.

Melanie Klein, Karen Horney, Margaret Mahler and other psychoanalysts contributed significantly to female developmental theory. Their observations, supported by studies of prenatal hormonal environments, newborns and infants, indicate that male/female psychological functions differ from birth and do not arise only during the

---

[59] These stages, first presented by Emma Jung in *Anima and Animus,* are amplified by Marie-Louise von Franz in "The Process of Individuation"; by Hilde Binswanger in "Positive Aspects of the Animus"; and by Claire Douglas in *The Woman in the Mirror,* chapters 6 and 7.

[60] *Female Authority: Empowering Women Through Psychotherapy.*

phallic stage as Freud proposed. Whether in terms of psychosexual drive or object-relations theory, the end of the second year (rapprochement subphase) not only marks the crisis of separation-individuation, but also is critical in the establishment of gender-identity.

Other revisions in Freudian theory regarding women are: 1) childbearing augments, but is not essential to, female identity (as a resolution to penis envy); 2) penis envy is normally resolved by the end of the oedipal period, not carried into adulthood; 3) a good relationship with mother during the separation-individuation phase of infancy and again in adolescence is crucial to female psychological development; 4) masochism is a factor in the psychodynamics of men and women, not limited to women.[61]

Jung's model too has been criticized for simplistically attributing Eros dominance to women and Logos dominance to men, and for its implicit acceptance of a secondary role for women in relationships, both within the family and in society. As we saw in chapter three, Jung's model is in the process of being reinterpreted.

Young-Eisendrath and Wiedemann adopted Loevinger's model of ego development in order to understand the assumptions a woman makes about herself. Loevinger's nine stages, arrived at by collecting data from women on a sentence-completion test over a twenty-five-year period, are as follows:

1) Presocial, in which symbiotic fusion with a mothering person constitutes the major form of relationship; in healthy chronological development, between conception and three to nine months;

2) Impulsive, in which a person assumes an external authority to be in control, acts impulsively and ambivalently in relationship through bodily states rather than verbal symbolic communication; approximately nine months to three years;

3) Self-Protective, an experience of individual agency and subjectivity, preoccupied with advantage and control in relationships; roughly three to six years;

4) Conformist, oriented around identity in a group, approval

---

[61] These are some of the findings reported by Eleanor Galenson for the American Psychoanalytic Association in "Psychology of Women."

seeking and meeting others' needs; ages seven to nineteen;

5) Self-Aware, a recognition of diversity of values and norms, struggling with independence but seeking approval from authority; a classic time to defer their identity crisis by forming an identity relationship with a man, about ages nineteen to twenty-eight;

6) Conscientious, in which personal achievement and responsibility are uppermost, empathy becomes possible, and cooperation and guilt may be prominent; any chronological period after late adolescence;

7) Individualistic stage, marked by an awareness of the essential nature of interdependence in human relating and by conflict between responsibility and creative freedom;

8) and 9) Autonomous and Integrating (combined by Young-Eisendrath and Wiedemann because of their relative infrequency), characterized by concerns with responsibilities, commitment to ideals of self-actualization, uniqueness, humor and imagination.

The developmental theories of Neumann and Loevinger lend themselves to a description of corresponding animus figures associated with each stage. Before presenting these, let us think about the significance of the stages in chronological development.

Since the personality is fluid, continually balancing different parts of the psyche called forth by various circumstances, it is possible for a woman to perform adequately in some situations while her undeveloped side remains in the background. Where close relationships with the opposite sex are concerned, we are all, men and women, particularly vulnerable. This is because of the numinous nature of archetypal energies when anima meets animus, and also because there are so few models of equal partner relationships. As we see in the Loevinger model, the achievement of an equal partnership is hard won. We may think of ourselves as quite adequate in our functioning, but still be relating at the earliest level in some situations. In other cases we may be ready for an equal partnership long before our mates are.

In analysis women learn to observe these movements in the psyche through attention to unconscious images and behavior, and to dialogue with the unconscious in a way that leads to further differentiation of its contents. The effect of this is the evolution of psychic images, such as a movement from alien animus figures to more positive animus figures, the expansion of possibilities in relatedness, and greater flexibility of ego. For example, in one woman's dream series we saw the progression of relationship to the animus from his appearance as alien intruder—fearful dreams of rapists and robbers, etc.—to bad little boy, to questionable politician, to philanthropist.

Young-Eisendrath and Wiedemann, observing in their patients' dreams and behavior the symbolic transformation of inner images which followed their progress through stages of development, describe typical animus images of each stage.

In the presocial stage the implicit animus figure is the Alien Outsider. He also characterizes the next four stages, but with a potential for violence at stage two, and with the beginnings of the patriarchal complex of Father, God or King at stage three. At the fourth stage of Conformist, there is still a strong unconscious identification of power with the mother archetype, but male authority may dominate action as the patriarchal complex is strengthened. The animus at the Self-Aware stage is typically patriarchal; there may be a preoccupation with power struggles in relationships but the notion of equality enters the picture as an ideal.

Young-Eisendrath and Wiedemann see the Hero animus emerging only with the fifth stage, the Conscientious. The ideal of mutuality in true partnership becomes possible, for the woman does not depend on a man to validate her own self-worth. The animus complex at the Individualistic stage is the Partner Within, the creative cooperation of animus and Self. In the last two stages the animus is fully integrated; the male-female polarity is united to form the androgyne with its full human potential.

Although Neumann does not specify animus figures to accompany his stages, implied are the complexes of Alien Outsider in the stages of Psychic Unity and Self-Conserving; Father, God or King at the stage of Self-Surrender; Hero at the stage of Patriarchal Partner, who rescues the feminine ego from the paternal uroboros; Partner Within during the stage of True Confrontation; and Androgyne at the final stage of the Experience of the Female Self.

To flesh out these animus types we may amplify as follows: the Alien Outsider includes stranger, rapist, abuser, abandoner, dwarf, monster, foreigner, animal; Father includes God, king, judge, president, corporate leader, professor, doctor, therapist, clergyman; Hero includes lover, leading man, sportsman, brother, guardian angel, rescuer, rock star, artist; Partner Within includes any equal partner, creative man, healer, magus, hierophant and transpersonal figure, but at a dimension of relatedness other than authoritarian; Androgyne presents itself in harmony with all living things.

The following section will present some different approaches to the classification of male figures in a woman's psyche.

Animus Types

One approach to knowing the animus, other than the developmental, is to look at archetypal patterns. Bearing in mind that archetypes cannot be known in themselves, but are reflected in movements of energy, we can examine these energy patterns in ourselves. Since they are neutral, and can be used for ill or good, archetypal figures have both positive and negative aspects.

Two writers who have expanded on archetypal patterns in men are Linda Leonard and Jean Shinoda Bolen. Leonard describes her encounters with inner figures, many of them male, on her journey of recovery from addiction.[62] Bolen personifies eight archetypal patterns, or "gods," which shape men's personalities and relationships.[63] Neither resorts to concepts of anima-animus, but both assert that men and women can experience these figures within.

Leonard tells us about the Demon Lover, who holds a woman hostage through denials that she is addicted and enthralled by him, and no longer makes decisions from her own center of survival, the Self. A woman who contains such an animus figure within may be attractive to, or attracted by, men who lead her into self-destructive behavior—physical, emotional or criminal.

The Moneylender offers ecstasy, but at such a high price that a person can never get out of debt to him, and so he controls the woman's life through her pursuit of the pleasure he offers and her feeling of guilt that she cannot repay him. Such an animus figure

---

[62] *Witness to the Fire: Creativity and the Veil of Addiction.*

[63] *Gods in Everyman: A New Psychology of Men's Lives and Loves.*

would have us bound by compulsive or guilt-ridden fixations.

The Gambler in us risks everything in the hope of an easy windfall; the stakes get higher as greater excitement is desired, until one is risking all. This can apply literally to actual gambling, or symbolically, a willingness to eschew reasonable priorities in order to chance it all for some elusive possibility.

The Romantic yearns for union with the beloved; while he carries the potential for the divine fire of creativity, untransformed he pulls us into death by suicide or addiction. We see the romantic animus prodding a woman to unrealistic behavior for the sake of an ideal, which in the perspective of a lifetime may be only a fleeting fancy .

The Underground Man, withholding and full of unexpressed resentment, kills the creativity in himself and others along with his rage. As an animus figure he provokes a woman to stingy, envious attitudes which greatly constrict possibilities of happiness, for both herself and those around her. But his narcissistic aura of importance can be magnetic.

The Outlaw, nursing a feeling of being different, must transform his rebelliousness through solidarity and creativity, or sink into what he resists, dependence on society. It is easy for women to project this antigroup attitude onto a man, and then become victimized by him and by society.

The Trickster, unpredictable wounder/healer, can open us to the divine or lead us to death through denial. Potentially creative, he must be acknowledged as a source of mischief in the psyche; otherwise his desire for turbulence damages everything a woman touches.

The Judge, in his role of patriarchal divider of dark and light, severs our connections with the instinctual life. The rational types, strong thinkers or feelers, are prone to this kind of animus and to ignoring important data from the body.

The Killer, driven by power and greed, loses all connection with the inner child and the nurturing feminine. Not content with winning the point, he wants to utterly demolish the other, and sadly, that other can be one's closest loved ones.

Leonard also describes one unambiguously female character, the Madwoman, who, enraged by neglect, accompanies the Judge in his repressed feminine underside. We will come again to the Madwoman in the discussion of anger and creativity. Here Leonard is differentiating animus types that figure in addiction in negative ways. A more positive relationship to the animus may flourish once the addiction is confronted.

Bolen classifies her animus figures according to their counterparts in the Greek pantheon, in two categories, fathers and sons. Aspects of the father archetype are Zeus, representing the realm of will and power; Poseidon, the realm of emotion and instinct; and Hades, the realm of souls and the unconscious. Aspects of the son are Apollo, the Sun God (who can also be considered a father type); Hermes, messenger and guide of souls, the Trickster archetype; Ares, God of War, the Warrior/Lover archetype; Hephaestus, craftsman and inventor, also an aspect of the father archetype or the Divine Child in its rejected, underground state; Dionysus, God of Ecstasy, a reflection of the Divine Child archetype.

Bolen writes:

> When the Great Goddess in her several aspects was the Mother God, fatherhood was not important, possibly not even recognized. When the Sky Father gods established patriarchal supremacy, the pendulum swung the other way: goddess and women were subjugated, which has been the historical and theological condition for several thousand years now. Male Gods have had dominion, and none of them either in Greek mythology or Judeo-Christianity has had both a strong and wise mother and a powerful and loving father. Few humans have, either.[64]

The Sky Father is in thrall to power; he is distant and jealous of his children and unrelated to the feelings of his wife. But the effect of the father archetype is slowly changing as individual men become more related to their women and children. Bolen anticipates the emergence of "the missing god"—a father god who is wise and loving, not power driven—in response to the growing presence in the world of the wisdom of the Goddess. The loving sons, Jesus in the West and Krishna in the East, have not changed the basic structure of the patriarchy, but they have provided a direction.

Archetypes do not change. But clearly their manifestations change

---

[64] Ibid., p. 295.

as human consciousness evolves. The emanation of the father archetype which Bolen calls the missing god has yet to have his day in the sun. Quoting Bolen again:

> It's been my impression that we all come into the world as children who want love, and if we can't get love, we settle for power. When we remember Metis (Goddess of Wisdom), we remember that love is what we really wanted all along.[65]

It is with the arrival of the missing god in mind that I explore the animus in women. It may be that we do not have to struggle till old age to be able to form deeply satisfying relationships with men, and to provide loving parenting to the children we bear in the world, as well as to the Divine Child inside.

---

[65] Ibid., p. 304.

6

Animus in the Body

They told me
I smile prettier with my mouth closed.
They said—
better cut your hair—
long, it's all frizzy,
looks Jewish.
—Jean Tepperman, from "Witch."

The tendency to view various parts of the body as masculine or feminine is ancient, as is obvious in those languages which require a gender-article before the noun: *le nez, la bouche, die hand, der finger.* Jungian analyst C.A. Meier has traced the history of dream interpretation, including ideas of the second-century Greek philosopher Artemidorus, who interpreted the head as "father," the right hand as masculine, and the left hand and pudendum as feminine.[66] Other systems see whole areas of the body in terms of gender; most frequently the left side is associated with the feminine.

All interpretations are subject to individual differences, so it is important to know a person's associations to dream images and other unconscious material. Still, sometimes generalizations can be useful as guidelines, or ways of amplifying personal associations.

In working with the body as an expression of psyche, I have found it useful to think of it in terms of four quadrants. I am grateful to Malcolm Brown for this concept,[67] which he adapted from D.H. Lawrence's *Phantasia of the Unconscious.* Brown writes:

> There are four regions of the body which mediate distinct modes of feeling-cognitive subject-world contact. The four regions are: the chest, the belly, the upper back, and the lower back. The chest re-

---

[66] *The Meaning and Significance of Dreams,* p. 166.
[67] *The Healing Touch,* p. 43.

71

gion includes the face and throat and extends to the diaphragm; the belly region includes the entire abdominal cavity and genitalia; the upper back region includes the cerebral cortex (or back half of the head), the two arms and hands; and the lower back region includes the legs and feet.

To summarize the mediation of these regions in my own words, the two front centers are affiliative centers and the back are will centers. I think of them in terms of yin-yang energies. As mentioned in an earlier chapter, yin can be conceived of as having a unique energy, not as *without* energy. The front top region of the body I see as yin-yang (primarily yin, secondarily yang); the energy is essentially receptive but flowing outward. The bottom front region is yin-yin; here too the energy is receptive but flows toward the center. The top back region is yang-yang; the energy is assertive and flows outward. The bottom back region is yang-yin; the energy is primarily assertive but flows toward the center.

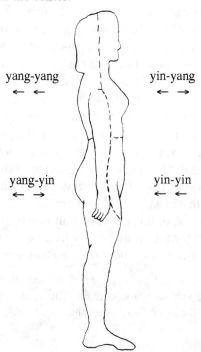

The four dynamic body centers

The front top (Brown calls it Eros) mediates sympathetic feelings, fusion or empathy. The front bottom (Brown calls it Hara) mediates homeostatic continuity of self-esteem and identity. The back top (Brown calls it Logos) mediates interaction and self-assertion; the back bottom (Brown calls it Spiritual Warrior) mediates determination and perseverance.

This schema inclines me to look for collective animus issues when the body or dreams show distress related to the head (top and back), back of the neck, shoulders, arms or upper back. These areas especially are subject to problems in dealing with the masculine in the outer world. With the lower back, the animus issues are more likely to be private ones having to do with personal goals and a sense of direction in life. The front half rarely involves animus integration; in women it is more likely to reflect questions about mothering, feminine identity and the expression of intimate feelings.

"The will to change begins in the body, not in the mind. My politics is in my body," says Adrienne Rich, "accruing and expanding with every act of resistance and each of my failures."[68]

Recently a woman brought this dream to her analytic session:

> I look out of a window and see my mother. There's something wrong with her head and back. She says she is going to lose the crown and top third of her head. She bent over for me to see. Her hair on the crown was very thin. Her doctor had told her there was some disease there which caused the problem. Mama turned, and I could see medical pen marks which showed the areas the doctor would remove. Outlined was the top of her head, down her back on both sides and along the waistline, which made the surgery run from the top of her head down her back to the waist. It seemed that what was removed (skin) would be replaced with something else.

Let us look at this dream using the classical Jungian method of dream analysis.[69] I think the term "dream interpretation" is somewhat misleading. It suggests that dreams are malleable and knowable, and can be tied down to a rational perspective. Although we do

---

[68] From "Tear Gas," *Poems: Selected and New, 1950-1974*, p. 140.

[69] See James A. Hall, *Jungian Dream Interpretation: A Handbook of Theory and Practice*, and Mary Ann Mattoon, *Applied Dream Analysis: A Jungian Approach*.

translate and find meaning in dream symbolism, it is wise to approach dreams with an attitude of circling, feeling through, relating to, living with.

To establish the dream context, we gather the dreamer's personal associations:

Window and *setting of the window:* no associations.

Thin hair: "Age twelve or early teens. I wanted to put my hair in rollers at night. Mama tried to stop me, because she believed rollers had made her hair thin on top; she had been told by her beautician not to sleep with rollers. I didn't listen, but didn't lose my hair. I did what I wanted, but she gave me a hard time . . . always at odds over her authority and my independence."

Head: "Something taken off my mother's thinking part."

Back: "Maybe something off *my* back; some discomfort or disease I've gotten from Mama."

Change: "A good change, something diseased removed; maybe superficial but it needed to come off. She always wanted to protect me from pain, especially pain from men. Her way was, 'Don't do anything'—withdraw and avoid. I've not done that with George."

Removing something from head and back: "Have to keep myself on an even keel and not think the worst; take things off my back and not carry them around."

Feeling state: "This feels like a positive change."

Another aspect of the context is the dreamer's psychological environment. This woman, divorced and in her late thirties, has been in analysis for about six months. She had stopped seeing a lover of two years a few months before the dream. Recently she met a separated man who was very attentive at first, but who decided to stop dating and consider returning to his marriage. She has been depressed over both these relationships, which she perceived as rejections. Her dilemma at the time of the dream was largely about whether to pursue contact with either of these men. She lives alone, has minimal contact with her mother, is physically healthy and attractive, has women friends and a good job, but longs for a heterosexual relationship. She is unsure of how to act, afraid of handling things badly.

A third aspect of the dream context is its archetypal parallels and symbolic associations. Relevant here would be rituals of scalping, particularly as a way of dealing with intruders, and shaving of the head, a form of renunciation of pleasure and a sign of asceticism. Hair in general is associated with thoughts and ideas. Cutting it off can symbolize getting rid of unconscious assumptions. Hair is also associated with sexuality, and cutting it can symbolize castration or depotentiation. Head and back, in my schema described above, are in the yang-yang area, suggesting collective animus issues. The window view may signify a perspective from a distance, without the need for close interaction—a place to consider possibilities before coming to a decision.

Jungian analysis also considers whether a dream is one of a particular series; in fact, it was one of several recent dreams about her mother. Then one looks at whether the dream refers to objective or subjective events. Since the mother is not under a doctor's care and has little direct impact on the dreamer's life, the dream can be seen as a commentary on the woman's subjective state. Finally, one looks at what compensatory function the dream may serve; for instance, how does it relate to the conscious experience of mother?

Since the dreamer is aware of certain negative effects of her relationship with mother and is trying to change old behavior patterns, the dream seems to confirm her conscious attitude. She describes herself as being "more accepting of myself . . . getting away from the old perfectionist stuff." By this she means that she has allowed herself to contact the men when she feels the need to, rather than withdraw completely, and also that she doesn't give herself a hard time for having done or not done something in the "right" way, the way a woman "should" in order to look good—as she felt her mother would encourage her to.

We explored her mother's relationship to the animus by examining her mother's attitude toward men in general, and particularly the dreamer's father and brother. The dreamer still feels great pain about family tension in her childhood and the constant fighting between her parents. Her father was jealous and possessive, her mother easily victimized. The reductive work that needs to be done concerns these early relationships, the damage to her self-confidence, assertiveness and feminine ground of being.

Looking at the dream from the perspective of the body, it suggests that the upper back carries the tension of repressed aggression which could be used in relating to the world, but which instead is withheld and experienced as depression.

In terms of animus development, the dreamer has come beyond the idealization of father and is struggling in the stage of the patriarchal partner. She has a good intellectual grasp of the next stage, but has not had the emotional experience necessary to fully actualize her independence and empowerment in relation to the masculine world. This may come, but one indication of her inadequate animus support is her fear of enduring depression without the help of medication.

A characteristic of a good relationship to the animus is the capacity to contain strong emotions. Containing, not repressing, painful depressive feelings entails facing the fact that she will cry a lot, become obsessive, perhaps lose sleep and weight, or possibly sleep too much or gain weight, depending on her physiology, and that this will all be very uncomfortable and distressing, but *all right*. She must trust that with the help of time, therapy, friendships and faith, she will become stronger and more comfortable, perhaps even happy. Of course nothing is guaranteed. Personally, what I hope for is that my analysands will discover more choices and more feelings, become more aware and authentic, and find more meaning in their lives.

A subjective dream of mother usually prompts me to inquire about the analysand's recent feelings about me and where she or he places me in terms of the internal struggle with an overprotective, victimized mother. In this case, the woman's response was that she saw me as a helper, but on the sidelines; not directing, but also not protecting her enough. She said she would prefer me to be more mothering, as another therapist had been. She wanted me to hold her and tell her everything would be okay. This she never had from her mother, and her previous therapy experience was brief.

Acknowledging this, she became tearful and once again the lonely child who had never received physical affection, whose feelings of fear in the face of continual discord between parents had never been received, and who had never been reassured and comforted. At this point, I felt it more important to hear her feelings than to gratify them. To hold her at this point would decrease her tension and interrupt the beginning self-examination process. Here is one of those times when an analyst holds symbolically, by listening and empathy, and waits for the process to deepen as the person struggles with accepting and containing loneliness.

The question of when to intervene in analysis with body contact is extremely complex, as I have discussed elsewhere.[70] Touching is my favorite metaphor for psychotherapy; in analysis I believe our purpose is to touch, especially those parts of the psyche that the patient feels to be "untouchable." Though healing takes place in analysis, it is not the analyst's purpose to heal. We risk inflation in seeing ourselves as healers, which implies that we are more whole than the patient. About that we can never be sure. Our purpose is not to change, not to fix, but only to touch . . . to reach beneath the armor, beneath the earth, down among the roots of being, to touch the buried moods, poems, dreams, the seeds of soaring possibilities.

With this woman, body therapy is a consideration for the future. At present, we are focusing on her own attention to her body.

> . . . they buttoned me into dresses
> covered with pink flowers.
> . . . I have been invisible,
> wierd and supernatural
> I want my black dress.
> I want my hair
> curling wild around me.[71]

I believe that both touch deprivation and inappropriate touching reflect problems in accepting the feminine. In some cultures children are teased, prodded and provoked to toughen them for life's physical hardships. Those exposed to rough and tumble horseplay and lots of body contact are generally relaxed and physically comfortable, but the line between play and abuse is thin and often crossed by adults. What children do to each other is seldom so damaging. A patient who as a child was tickled intensely by her father, in the name of fun, found it was associated with sexual abuse on the inner level. Because so much ambivalence arises around body contact, sexual behavior often substitutes for affection and affirmation, at any age.

---

[70] See *Touching: Body Therapy and Depth Psychology.*

[71] Jean Tepperman, from "Witch," *No More Masks,* pp. 333-334.

Adrienne Rich wrote of becoming aware of her father's body:

My father's tense, narrow body did not seize my imagination,
though authority and control ran through it like electric filaments. I
used to glimpse his penis dangling behind a loosely tied bathrobe.
But I had understood very early that he and my mother were different.
It was his voice, presence, style, that seemed to pervade the household. I don't remember when it was that my mother's sensuousness,
the reality of her body, began to give way for me to the charisma of
my father's assertive mind and temperament; perhaps when my sister
was just born and he began teaching me to read.[72]

It is the inseparability of body and spirit that makes it impossible
to define the nuances that determine our gender preferences.

Mary Oliver reminds us of the body as incarnated spirit:

The spirit
     likes to dress up like this:
          ten fingers,
               ten toes,

shoulders, and all the rest
     at night
          in the black branches,
               in the morning

in the blue branches
     of the world.
          It could float, of course,
               but would rather

plumb rough matter.
     Airy and shapeless thing,
          it needs
               the metaphor of the body,

lime and appetite,
     the oceanic fluids;
          it needs the body's world
               instinct

and imagination

---

[72] *Of Woman Born: Motherhood As Experience and Institution,* p. 219.

and the dark hug of time,
    sweetness
        and tangibility,

to be understood,
    to be more than pure light
        that burns
            where no one is—

so it enters us—
    in the morning
        shines from brute comfort
            like a stitch of lightning;

and at night
    lights up the deep and wondrous
        drownings of the body
            like a star.[73]

Marge Piercy writes intimately and with exquisite fluidity about the human body:

Cats like angels are supposed to be thin;
pigs like cherubs are supposed to be fat.
People are mostly in between, a knob
of bone sticking out in the knee you might
like to pad, a dollop of flab hanging
over the belt. You punish yourself,
one of those rubber balls kids have
that come bouncing back off their own
paddles, rebounding on the same slab.
You want to be slender and seamless
as a bolt.
           When I was a girl
I loved spiny men with ascetic grimaces
all elbows and words and cartilage
ribbed like cast up fog-grey hulls,
faces to cut the eyes blind
on the glittering blade, chins
of Aegean prows bent on piracy.

---

[73] "Poem," *Dream Work,* pp. 52-53.

Now I look for men whose easy bellies
show a love for the flesh and the table,
men who will come in the kitchen
and sit, who don't think peeling potatoes
makes their penis shrink; men with broad
fingers and purple figgy balls,
men with rumpled furrows and the slightly
messed look at ease of beds recently
well used.
               We are not all supposed
to look like undernourished fourteen year
old boys, no matter what the fashions
ordain. You are built to pull a cart,
to lift a heavy load and bear it,
to haul up the long slope, and so
am I, peasant bodies, earthy, solid
shapely dark glazed clay pots that can
stand on the fire. When we put our
bellies together we do not clatter
but bounce on the good upholstery.[74]

One of the ways a negative relationship to the animus works destructively in a woman is by taking her out of her body. This can happen in a number of ways. She can be possessed with a perfectionism that leads her to subject her body to harsh and even abusive treatment for the sake of some external goal; for example, anorexia acquired in the attempt to look a certain way, ignoring the inner states of hunger and tension. We can picture the energy distribution in the anorexic body as top-heavy and ungrounded. All the focus of energy is on the upper realm of thinking, planning, controlling.[75]

In other cases, the drive to control takes the energy right out and up into intellectual pursuits or "airy" issues of some kind. The body is ignored, allowed to become flabby, weak, sick, stiff or numb. A preoccupation with anything that closes off attention to the body

---

[74] "Cats Like Angels," *Circles on the Water,* pp. 255-256.

[75] See Marion Woodman, *The Owl Was a Baker's Daughter: Obesity, Anorexia Nervosa and the Repressed Feminine,* and *Addiction to Perfection: The Still Unravished Bride.*

means a refusal to listen to one's feminine ego, even when the preoccupation is something that appears feminine, such as "looking pretty" or mothering others.

The inner male can be so critical of spontaneity or sexuality that repressive thought processes cut off any feelings arising from the body. Or the criticism may come in the form of shameful feelings about asking for help, the need to be self-sufficient and strong, even if it kills her (and it might). As mentioned above in regard to addiction, the inner male can seduce a woman into ignoring her body in order to pursue a pleasure or gratify some infantile fixation. There is no simple summarizing of male/female energies in the critical choices concerning pregnancy, this core of life-death decisions.[76]

Marilyn Nagy contends that good psychological development in women depends on a continual dialectic between introversion and extraversion. In the first half of the menstrual cycle, according to Nagy, women are more outer-oriented and influenced by the collective. In the second half of the cycle, and during pregnancy and later life, there is increased introversion.[77] These cyclical movements can be supported by the animus; although we more often think of the animus as outward bound, the animus as psychopomp can at these times encourage introversion.

A forty-year-old woman, married, had successfully forged herself a niche in a world of powerful businessmen through intelligence and dedication, without benefit of a college education. She was one of two daughters of a cruelly strict father and a submissive, frightened mother. The children dreaded hearing his step when he returned from work in the evening, and cowered before his angry perfectionism. This woman came for help because her body was racked by tension headaches which were getting worse. Her sister had been diagnosed as schizophrenic and could barely function outside of an institution. Gradually, through analysis of her relationship to her father, concurrent with body therapy, her symptoms diminished.

What was remarkable to me was the discipline with which this woman denied pain. Her headaches had to become crippling before

---

[76] See Christina Cutts, "When Logic Fails," and Sue Nathanson, *Soul Crisis: One Woman's Journey Through Abortion to Renewal.*

[77] "Menstruation and Shamanism."

she attempted to treat them. She also suffered from other painful symptoms which she could manage to turn off all day while she worked at her job; then, at home in the evening, she would suffer. This is a form of possession by the negative animus. The creative woman can be seized by the positive animus as well, ignoring her body in order to reach for ever higher goals.

Often the inner messages involved in these destructive behaviors come from the mother, not necessarily the men in a woman's life. However, on closer examination it is invariably the mother's need to propitiate some masculine power that is being foisted upon the daughter—an overconcern for "what the neighbors think" or with status in the community, or some other abstract goal.

For so long and so insidiously have our bodies been subjugated, as objects or possessions, to masculine values, that we have trouble imagining what a truly supportive environment for women would look like. Women's gatherings try to create this, to compensate for centuries of being made to feel shame over menstrual blood, a privilege which warrants the reverence of ritual and celebration; years of giving over our birthing processes to the impersonal masculine medical model; of valuing the shape of the breast more than the pleasure of creating and nursing a baby; of believing that we can only have worth with this kind of neck, nose or knee; of having fashion-czars exalt a body which looks more like that of a young boy than a mature woman; of believing that men with gray hair and facial lines can be sexually attractive, but women cannot.

In the context of warm-body-mothering which is supported, not distorted, by the animus, the mother-dominated stage gives a strong foundation to values of comfort, being at ease with the earthy, physical world and its nurturant pleasures, wonder and respect for the physiological functions, pride in the moon rounds of feminine mystery, the capacity to let go and trust *being* to take over.

When the father's influence becomes dominant and inspiration supercedes nurturing, a new perspective arises that allows us to postpone and curtail the literal taking-in in favor of receiving spiritually. We gain some control over the natural processes—exercise regimes, physical fitness, etc. We can anticipate the physical future and plan for it. Awareness of the hero brings the narcissistic self to the fore, allowing us to face the issues of survival of the fittest on a social and sexual level. The absence of animus support at these stages is seen in obesity, anorexia, bulimia and addictions; infertility, stress-disorders, psychosomatic illnesses; premenstrual and menstrual disorders, and sexual disfunction.

At the stage of equal partners in our society there is a relaxing of efforts to create the correct body, and an appreciation for the natural functions and natural beauty. There may be problems as the effects of lifelong neglect begin to show up, or stress and the strains of age appear, and genetic factors become most apparent.

Cultural attitudes toward the body have gone through several recent transformations. In the previous century it was fashionable to view the body as a machine; later, as a child; and now, the body is often identified with the feminine. This is understandable, for the body was so denigrated, along with the feminine, during the patriarchal dominance of Western civilization, that both were relegated to the collective shadow. Feminine wisdom, which is closely related to body wisdom, and the wisdom of the unconscious, were ignored.

Now, as the feminine becomes more integrated into collective consciousness, we tend to identify body, feminine and unconscious as equivalent. While this is a step forward from ignoring all three, it still reflects our incomplete psychic development , which must eventually recognize body wisdom as an expression of the Self, both/neither masculine and/nor feminine.

7
Anger and Creativity

There's in my mind a woman
of innocence, unadorned but

fair-featured, and smelling of
apples or grass. She wears

a utopian smock or shift, her hair
is light brown and smooth, and she

is kind and very clean without
ostentation—

        but she has
no imagination.
        And there's a
turbulent moon-ridden girl

or old woman, or both,
dressed in opals and rags, feathers

and torn taffeta,
who knows strange songs—

but she is not kind.

—Denise Levertov, "In Mind."

A woman had been struggling for over a year with physiological problems in her upper respiratory system and ears, and at times they were life threatening. Medical treatment would seem to bring the problems under control but they would return. The failure of medicine to cure her led to confusion and disagreements among her physicians. Asthma, sinus infections, yeast infections and auto-immune system illnesses were treated but nothing helped.

In the meantime she and I worked at clearing out psychological debris, which was considerable: fear and hatred stemming from childhood abuse and years of failing to establish secure intimate relationships. Copious tears were released by the attention to these years of courageous survival.

One night she had this dream:

A charming man is wrestling with my illness, which is in the form of a dragon. The man, in his early twenties, is beautiful. He has a gorgeous tan, bronze, and his body is strong without being muscle-bound. He has blond curls and he glistens. He is enjoying the battle, matching his strength against an opponent of this significance. The opponent, a dragon, is blue, scaly with an iridescent quality, almost like the sky. The young warrior is very confident and assured; he is laughing as he subdues the dragon. He is not killing it, but stuffing it into a huge container, making sure it has enough room. The dragon didn't need to be killed, but it needed to be contained, and he was putting it into this big round container, like a large cardboard commercial container.

This woman had not been aware of the controversy in feminist thought and literature about the nature of the tension between ego and unconscious. For years the only image we had of the emergence of the ego from the unconscious was a violent one. Whether in terms described by Eric Neumann (the slaying of the dragon) or by psychoanalytic writers (repression of unconscious contents by the superego), the process of ego emergence had been consistently pictured as the battle of masculine ego against feminine underworld.

Then the voices of women began to be heard in theoretical circles. These images did not reflect their experience of ego-formation. The development of ego could be imaged as a gradual process of differentiation, the result of trial and error, or shifts, occasionally leaps, to new territory. Nothing had to be killed; a previous state could be abandoned or outgrown. Though ego development was often the result of overcoming frustration, that was not the whole story. Even the overcoming of frustration did not necessarily imply the repression or killing off of unconscious contents. It might just as well derive from conscious choices made gradually and steadily over a period of time. The "diffuse" thinking stereotypically attributed to women began to seem more acceptable, even reasonable.

But most distressing to women was that what was being killed in order to attain wholeness was the feminine. While this is portrayed in

Neumann's theory as a temporary stage in the development of the psyche, until the hero (ego) can return to the scene of battle with greater awareness to recapture the now acceptable feminine which has been separated out from "Mother" (unconscious), it is still grating to the female viewpoint. Too often women, as partners of men embedded in the mother complex, have had to carry negative projections that led to abuse or abandonment. If their men were supposed to have knocked off the mother complex—slain the dragon—and come to them staunch, heroic and ready for mature relationship, something had gone awry. The process looked more like a continual hacking away at anything female.

Naturally this metaphor refers to an internal process and not necessarily to the actual mother-child relationship. What the hero must conquer is his own fear of separation, death and regression. Nevertheless, the drama is often expressed directly with the mother or partner carrying the heavy burden of the archetypal mother. Woman knows instinctively that she cannot kill any aspect of the feminine without doing damage to herself. She also recognizes that the longer metaphors like this are used with her consent, the longer she is likely to remain oppressed and devalued, and the more difficult it is for men to come to wholeness.

Neumann recognized that women's psychology required a different metaphor and wrote another version of the developmental process to explain ego development from the feminine vantagepoint. In that schema, described above in chapter five, woman remains connected to the Great Mother and experiences her development in terms of more and more differentiation of her relationship to the masculine. First, according to Neumann, she learns self-conserving attitudes which replace fusion with mother; then she allows herself to surrender to the patriarchal numinosum. Following this ecstatic surrender, which can be seen in the worshipful attitudes of three-year-old girls to their fathers, comes the transference of that positive attitude onto a peer. Ideally this partnership evolves from a patriarchal relationship to one of equality, and finally to realization of the female Self.

The problem is that no amount of development on the part of the woman will lead to true equality in a relationship unless the man is also willing to be open and intimate. For most men it is a very long journey from the killing of the dragon to the rescue of the captive princess—and even farther to their wedding.

Now, what was noteworthy in my patient's dream was her unconscious understanding of the need to keep the dragon alive and her appreciation of its beauty. This reflects the uniquely feminine capacity to view the enemy as valuable. This ability of women, so long denigrated by patriarchal attitudes as "fuzzy thinking" or "bleeding-heart mentality," is exactly what will be needed to insure survival of life in many forms, and, possibly, of the planet.

In the patient, this attitude colored her approach toward her illness in several ways. For example, although she accepted the use of antibiotics in the early stages of treatment, she soon rejected their continual use, out of an intuitive belief that what had not worked should not be continued. She believed that she was somehow damaging her capacity to recuperate by prolonged attempts to wipe out the problem with chemicals.

Some physicians saw her as uncooperative and self-destructive. Others saw her as understandably discouraged by a mode of therapy which did not appear to be having any lasting positive effect. They supported her investigation into alternative methods, and, in the course of "trying everything," my patient changed her lifestyle. Gradually she altered her workaholic schedule, her relationships, diet and habitual use of cigarettes, caffeine, alcohol and other substances to which she was found to have an allergic reaction. As the dream shows, she changed her inner world by facing the unpleasant facts that had been her history and shaped her choices.

It is interesting to note that her dragon-illness appeared in the dream as a sky-blue creature. I have seen this image in the dreams of other women, for example a blue lioness dug up from the ground, or a blue sphinx-like creature which terrifies and attracts at the same time. One interpretation of such an image is the union of earthiness and heavenliness; the creature comes from below but wears the colors of the sky, as does the Christian Madonna in most Western depictions (the Virgin Goddess in her blue cloak).

Why is the hero of this dream a young man? I believe this reflects the woman's stage of animus development. She has dealt with many mother issues, shadow issues and father issues, and is now in the process of finding her inner partner. In Neumann's schema, she was developing a relationship with the patriarchal partner. The dream hero, the golden man, is an emanation of Apollo, so to speak. They are not likely to make a permanently compatible couple, but he is an important ally on the way. At another stage of life the heroic animus might appear as a fairy godmother, a helpful animal, a father or Self figure. This hero in fact represents both animus and Self, because at present she becomes aware of the Self primarily in terms of animus projections. It is her work in relating to her animus which will bring her into relationship with her feminine Self.

While the dream hero is masculine, the opponent is neuter. Although men may project femininity onto the dragon, women are likely to see it as masculine. As the Great Unconscious (not only Great Mother but also Great Father), it is both all and nothing. The woman is reluctant to destroy it; her reaction is to contain it, to preserve its life, to live with it and, presumably, continue some relationship with it.

Why should she want to preserve her illness? That is a question I will not try to answer; I trust and respect it as an unsolved mystery. We know that the "force that drives the illness"[78] contains great energy. How that energy will be transformed is yet to unfold, but the dream was a turning point in that process and a turning point in her regaining her health.

Now, having presented this picture of the feminine tendency to sustain and preserve, where is there room for the destructive side? Self-acceptance implies containing all that one is capable of being, including the survivor's emotions of rage and murderousness. The following poem by Marge Piercy supports the life-giving effect on the body of acknowledging rage.

> Anger shines through me.
> Anger shines through me.
> I am a burning bush.
> My rage is a cloud of flame.
> My rage is a cloud of flame
> in which I walk

---

[78] This refers to Dylan Thomas's phrase, above, p. 36.

seeking justice
like a precipice.
How the streets
of the iron city
flicker, flicker,
and the dirty air
fumes.
Anger storms
between me and things,
transfiguring,
transfiguring.
A good anger acted upon
is beautiful as lightning
and swift with power.
A good anger swallowed,
a good anger swallowed
clots the blood
to slime.[79]

Paula Bennett, in her illuminating study of the psychological development of Emily Dickinson, Sylvia Plath and Adrienne Rich, as reflected in their poetry, follows these women in their tasks of self-definition and self-empowerment.

Their womanhood enables their verse and gives them their poetic power just as, traditionally, manhood and the masculine point of view have provided the focus, themes, and substance of the male poet's verse.[80]

Bennett points out that Emily Dickinson, in the following poem, presents herself "as everything 'woman' is not: cruel, not pleasant, hard not soft, emphatic not weak, one who kills, not one who nurtures. Just as significant, she is proud of it."[81]

My Life had stood—a Loaded Gun—
In Corners—till a Day
The Owner passed—identified—
And carried Me away—

---

[79] "A Just Anger," *Circles on the Water,* p. 88.
[80] *My Life a Loaded Gun,* p. 8.
[81] Ibid., p. 6.

And now We roam in Sovereign Woods—
And now We hunt the Doe—
And every time I speak for Him—
The Mountains straight reply—

And do I smile, such cordial light
Upon the Valley glow—
It is as a Vesuvius face
Had let its pleasure through—

And when at Night—Our good Day done—
I guard My Master's Head—
Tis better than the Eider-Duck's
Deep Pillow—to have shared—

To foe of His—I'm deadly foe—
None stir the second time—
On whom I lay a Yellow Eye—
Or an emphatic Thumb—

Though I than He—may longer live
He longer must—than I—
For I have but the power to kill,
Without—the power to die—[82]

Despite the ambivalence that comes through here, despite the conflict, writes Bennett,

> In the poem's terms, she is murderous. She is a gun. Her rage is part of her being. Indeed, insofar as it permits her to explode and hence to speak, rage defines her, unwomanly and inhuman though it is. Whatever constraints existed in her daily life . . . inwardly it would seem Emily Dickinson was not to be denied. In her art she was master of herself, whatever that self was, however aggressive, unwomanly, or even inhuman society might judge it to be.[83]

Although Dickinson's metaphor holds her "owner" to be male, we don't have to attribute rage to the animus. There is enough evidence that women are capable of rage entirely on their own; we would not claim Hecate, Medusa, Kali, Morrigu, Hera, Sekmet, Artemis or

---

[82] *The Poems of Emily Dickinson*, no. 754.
[83] *My Life a Loaded Gun*, p. 7.

Seboulisa to be animus-possessed. All human infants are born with this survival mechanism, but not necessarily with a love of combat and competition for its own sake. In the rage of each of these goddesses one finds the fundamental motive to be preservative, a "just anger," not a narcissistic exhibition of strength.

The rage of women expressed in modern poetry is mainly a colossal explosion which breaks through centuries of oppression, oppression that has stifled our individual creative energy and our natural compassion for the earth and all its creatures.

No matter what the target—Patriarchy, Man, Society; mothers who left us a legacy of masochism; fathers who denigrated them and all too often abandoned or cheated on them, husbands who disappointed us; gods, muses or some other abstract force—the rage must be seen and felt and heard before life can go on. In expressing themselves, women are speaking as well for generations of men whose creative urges were suppressed by the collective demand that they "pay the bills." They too have often had to deny their true needs.

It seems to be necessary for women to find their boiling-point, to know the limits of their patience and generosity and to feel beyond that limit, before they can fully experience their own right to be. Rather than seeing the capacity for rage as a masculine quality, I find the constraints on righteous rage by the negative animus—he who tells us to be good and quiet—to be behind more subtle forms of destruction of self and others. It is he whom Sylvia Plath addresses as "Herr God, Herr Lucifer" in her suicidal poem, "Lady Lazarus."

It is noteworthy, as we saw in chapter four, that so little has been written about the feminine aspects of the Divine. I find it no coincidence that so many modern women have written about the image of the Medusa, a figure personifying destructive rage. Bennett, in a collection of poetry which takes Medusa as its muse, describes how women, in reclaiming their "unladylike" capacity for passionate rage, also reclaim their full creativity and love.

By 1973 women poets came from virtually every walk of life and from every heretofore silenced minority: not just women of color, but lesbians, older women, working-class women, country women, prisoners, the poor, and, not without irony, mothers. No longer seeking "pardon for [their] literary pretensions," they saw in poetry a direct means by which to express and change their lives.[84]

The capacity for rage is necessary for women to proceed from a *participation mystique* with the mother-world to a more individualized stage of development. This by no means requires them to give up their capacity for empathy and compassion. This is rage expressed in the interest of extending life, not subjugating it. In this case the opposite of rage is cold indifference, a characteristic of Plath's "moon-mother-muse";[85] rage and compassion are allies. In establishing sovereignty over herself, woman gains the capacity to choose. Where once co-dependency was a compulsion, now dependency can become a creative choice.

It has been said of Sylvia Plath, "It needed not only great intelligence and insight to handle the material; it also took a kind of bravery. Poetry of this order is a murderous art."[86] She herself wrote, "What inner decision, what inner murder or prison break must I commit if I want to speak from my true deep voice?"[87]

I don't know if Plath thought of herself as brave. Her poetry expressed a pivotal point in women's development, poignantly portraying the polarity between affiliation and autonomy, and raising questions about the place of narcissism. Because her mother, Aurelia Plath, and her husband, Ted Hughes, have published her letters and journals, we have more material than is usually available to understand a writer.

Volumes have been written analyzing Plath's life and work. I would like to focus on one view of her poetry that seems to illustrate the dilemma facing modern women, which has been succinctly called the conflict between relation and creation. To state it as simply as possible, the stereotypical masculine is seen as assertive in the struggle for separation and autonomy, while the feminine is deemed to be nurturing, longing for attachment and caring. Feminists are not in

---

[84] Ibid. pp. 242-243. Medusa-inspired poems have been penned by May Sarton, Louise Bogan, Karen Lindsey, Rachel Blau DuPlessis, Audre Lorde, Colleen J. McElroy and Chrystos, to name a few.

[85] Ibid., p. 160.

[86] A. Alvarez, *The Review* (quoted on the back cover of *Ariel*).

[87] *The Journals of Sylvia Plath,* p. 297.

agreement as to what the main thrust of their message should be. On one hand, there seems to be some evidence that the stereotype is at least partly true; women should recognize that their need for affiliation is not a weakness, but a tremendous strength whose time has come, perhaps not too late to save the world. On the other hand, creativity, other than that involved in caring for children, requires separateness and autonomy, and, if a woman's worth is not to depend solely on caretaking, she has a right to her necessary separateness, as do men.

To understand the part played by these dynamics in Plath's work it is helpful to contrast her tortured and unacceptable self-image with her need to present herself, socially and in her letters to her family, in the most pleasant and optimistic light. The disparity between her sugar-coated letters (about seven hundred in all) and her obsidian poetry is astounding. Bennett says that she was in conflict "between the needs of her gender and the requirements of her genre."[88]

The reaction of some critics to Plath's poetry illustrates the core problem. Because of the raw intensity of her emotion, and because her message flows through very personal, often domestic images—body parts, kitchen knives, food, babies, etc.—she has been taken less than seriously by some, who imply that her writing was not transcendent, only a self-serving form of confessional therapy. However, some critics see Plath's domestic and mythical images in terms of historical and social issues, suggesting that her femininity and her suicide prevent some men from being able to see their full meaning.[89]

Both Emily Dickinson and Sylvia Plath came from conservative backgrounds with selflessly caring mothers and distinguished fathers. Bennett feels that Dickinson was able to break the bond with mother, as illustrated in "My Life a Loaded Gun," but that Plath was never able to sacrifice the goal of normalcy that mother and society held up for her. Trying to be the perfect student, as well as popular and successful, she achieved them all for a while. Her mother, an in-

---

[88] *My Life a Loaded Gun,* p. 99.

[89] See, for instance, Lynda Bundtzen, *Plath's Incarnations: Woman and the Creative Process,* and Judith Kroll, *Chapters in Mythology: The Poetry of Sylvia Plath,* pp. 1-13.

telligent, ambitious woman, attained masters degrees in English and German, then married her professor, Otto Plath, and devoted herself to supporting his writing and caring for their two children. Sylvia's first recorded disappointment occurred when she was two and a half, and her brother was born:

> Sometimes I nursed starfish alive in jam jars of seawater and watched them grow back lost arms. On this day, this awful birthday of otherness, my rival, somebody else, I flung the starfish against a stone. Let it perish.[90]

In 1940, when Sylvia was eight, Otto Plath died of willfully neglected diabetes.

Sylvia was brilliant and conscientious. In spite of outstanding early success, she suffered several severe depressions, one being during the summer after her junior year at Smith College. She had experienced disappointments and was back home with her mother. Surviving a suicide attempt, she returned to and graduated from Smith in 1955 with highest honors. Her mother, recovering from surgery for ulcers developed while nursing her husband through his fatal illness, managed to attend the graduation in her semi-invalid state. Sylvia went to Cambridge as a Fullbright scholar where she competed fiercely for approval as a poet and as a woman. In one of her journals she distinguishes between approval and love. Writing about her mother, she said: "Why is telling her of a success so unsatisfying: because one success is never enough. When you love you have an indefinite lease of it. When you approve you only approve single acts."[91]

Her preoccupation with marrying an attractive, successful husband led to her idealized marriage to poet Ted Hughes. Plath's sense of accomplishment at this event, and her blatant delight at having pleased her mother, is obvious in her journals. "My life work is to make Ted into the best man the world has seen."[92] That she perceived a split between being intellectual and being a woman is also

---

[90] "Ocean 1212W," *Johnny Panic and the Bible of Dreams*, p. 23.

[91] *The Journals of Sylvia Plath*, p. 281.

[92] Paula Bennett, *My Life a Loaded Gun*, p. 162.

obvious, and not at all unusual for her time. Here we see the importance she had come to place on marriage in terms of self-affirmation:

> Two girls there are: within the house
> One sits; the other, without.
> Daylong a duet of shade and light
> Plays between these.
>
> In her dark wainscoted room
> The first works problems on
> A mathematical machine.
> Dry ticks mark time
>
> As she calculates each sum.
> At this barren enterprise
> Rat-shrewd go her squint eyes,
> Root-pale her meager frame.
>
> Bronzed as earth, the second lies,
> Hearing ticks blown gold
> Like pollen on bright air. Lulled
> Near a bed of poppies,
>
> She sees how their red silk flare
> Of petalled blood
> Burns open to sun's blade.
> On that green altar
>
> Freely become sun's bride, the latter
> Grows quick with seed.
> Grass-couched in her labor's pride,
> She bears a king. Turned bitter
>
> And sallow as any lemon,
> The other, wry virgin to the last,
> Goes graveward with flesh laid waste,
> Worm-husbanded, yet no woman.[93]

Marriage to Hughes was heady, but the idealizations began to fade with the birth of her two children. Living in England, Plath was isolated and duty-bound while Hughes pursued his career and enjoyed the spotlight as well as the attention of bright younger women. Two

---

[93] "Two Sisters of Persephone," *Collected Poems,* pp. 31-32.

months after the birth of her first child, Frieda, she wrote:

> By the roots of my hair some god got hold of me.
> I sizzled in his blue volts like a desert prophet.
>
> The nights snapped out of sight like a lizard's eyelid:
> A world of bald white days in a shadeless socket.
>
> A vulturous boredom pinned me in this tree.
> If he were I, he would do what I did.[94]

Plath's poetry at that time shows that she felt stultified and confined, both by the physical constraints typical for a new mother and by her perception of herself as nonproductive artistically. Some of her images suggest the mental constraints were the more burdensome. The conflict between the masculine carriers of Logos and her feminine, concrete tasks is apparent still in "Magi":

> The abstracts hover like dull angels:
> Nothing so vulgar as a nose or an eye
> Bossing the ethereal blanks of their face-ovals.
>
> Their whiteness bears no relation to laundry,
> Snow, chalk, or such-like. They're
> The real thing, all right: The Good, the True—
>
> Salutary and pure as boiled water,
> Loveless as the multiplication table.
> While the child smiles into thin air.
>
> Six months in the world, and she is able
> To rock on all fours like a padded hammock.
> For her, the heavy notion of Evil
>
> Attending her cot is less than a belly ache,
> And Love, the mother of milk, no theory.
> They mistake their star, these papery godfolk.
>
> They want the crib of some lamp-headed Plato.
> Let them astound his heart with their merit.
> What girl ever flourished in such company?[95]

---

[94] "The Hanging Man," ibid., p.141.

[95] Ibid., p. 148.

In 1960 her poetry began to reveal more of her true feelings; images of the dark mother-moon-muse were coming through and the split between the good girl and the angry victim was narrowing.

> Mother, mother, what illbred aunt
> Or what disfigured and unsightly
> Cousin did you so unwisely keep
> Unasked to my christening, that she
> Sent these ladies in her stead
> With heads like darning-eggs to nod
> And nod and nod at foot and head
> And at the left side of my crib?
>
> . . . .
>
> Day now, night now, at head, side, feet,
> They stand their vigil in gowns of stone,
> Faces blank as the day I was born,
> Their shadows long in the setting sun
> That never brightens or goes down.
> And this is the kingdom you bore me to,
> Mother, mother. But no frown of mine
> Will betray the company I keep.[96]

In "Medusa," we feel the cloying persistence of the clutching mother, determined to hold on, even with an ocean between them. Although aspects of her mother seem to have invited this projection, the responsibility for understanding it lay ultimately with Plath.

> Off that landspit of stony mouth-plugs,
> Eyes rolled by white sticks,
> Ears cupping the sea's incoherences,
> You house your unnerving head—God-ball,
> Lens of mercies,
>
> . . . .
>
> Who do you think you are?
> A Communion wafer? Blubbery Mary?
> I shall take no bite of your body,
> Bottle in which I live,

---

[96] "The Disquieting Muses," ibid., pp. 75-76.

Ghastly Vatican.
I am sick to death of hot salt.
Green as eunuchs, your wishes
Hiss at my sins.
Off, off, eely tentacle!

There is nothing between us.[97]

According to Judith Kroll, Plath was influenced by Jung's theory that parents, while attempting to do their best for their children, usually thrust onto them what they have neglected in themselves.[98] To put it another way, children unconsciously live out their parents' shadows, and often, through resentment, repeat their failures.

In her analysis of "Medusa," Bundtzen notes that Plath's mother's name, Aurelia, is synonymous with *medusa,* the adult stage in the life of a jellyfish. Bundtzen speculates that Aurelia's visit during Plath's marital crisis, and her witnessing of Hughes' infidelity, impressed Plath with the image of the gaze that turns one to stone, prompting the irrational but psychologically seductive notion that mother saw, and caused, the failure of the marriage.[99]

The dual images, jellyfish and Gorgon, underline the devouring and paralyzing nature of any symbiotic relationship. Separated from Hughes, Plath is flung back into the world of mother where she must relive the complex set of conflicts attending the mother-daughter bond and all its frightening ramifications—dependency, envy and fear of annihilation. Concurrently, she includes religious themes as well, amplifying her ambivalence and reflecting her failure to find a spiritual solution to her feeling of entrapment.

At this point, the unrealistically optimistic mother of the earlier poems seems to have less and less weight, and the disquieting muses take on more and more power. In "The Moon and the Yew Tree," for instance, the moon is reminiscent of the muses referred to in "The Disquieting Muses"—stony, bald, wild, inimical and indifferent to her earthy needs:

---

[97] Ibid., pp. 225-226.
[98] *Chapters in Mythology: The Poetry of Sylvia Plath,* pp. 74-76.
[99] *Plath's Incarnations: Woman and the Creative Process,* pp. 89-109.

This is the light of the mind, cold and planetary.
The trees of the mind are black. The light is blue.
. . . .
It drags the sea after it like a dark crime; it is quiet
with the O-gape of complete despair. I live here.[100]

About this time Plath wrote her mother in glowing terms about her
new hairdo and clothes, her plan to paint the bedrooms, Frieda's
blossoming in the company of other children, her son Nick's happiness: "How lucky I am to have two beautiful babies and work!"[101]
Meanwhile she was devastated about Hughes' affair with another
woman. Within a month, she killed herself by putting her head in the
gas oven of her kitchen. Here is her last poem:

The woman is perfected.
Her dead

Body wears the smile of accomplishment,
The illusion of a Greek necessity

Flows in the scrolls of her toga,
Her bare

Feet seem to be saying:
We have come so far, it is over.

Each dead child coiled, a white serpent,
One at each little

Pitcher of milk, now empty.
She has folded

Them back into her body as petals
Of a rose close when the garden

Stiffens and odours bleed
From the sweet, deep throats of the night flower.

The moon has nothing to be sad about,
Staring from her hood of bone.

She is used to this sort of thing.
Her blacks crackle and drag.[102]

---

100 *Collected Poems*, p.173.
101 *Letters Home: Correspondence 1950-63.*, p. 580.
102 "Edge," *Collected Poems*, p. 273.

Here, and in several of her other last poems—"Ariel" and "Stings," for example[103]—Plath seems to have determined to entomb the feminine, tolerated by the moon-muse only in its most negative aspects, sexual sterility and death. Bennett writes:

> For Plath to achieve autonomy meant that she had to destroy the dependent, attachment-prone side of herself. Once that self was destroyed, however, all that remained was a woman too wicked to live.[104]

> Caught in a culture that devalued and disempowered her as a woman and bound to a mother who was never able to achieve the sense of separation and autonomy needed to help herself, let alone her daughter, Sylvia Plath burnt herself out in rage.[105]

Bennett discusses the conflict women writers experience in having to expose themselves and points out that though few have committed suicide, many have destroyed their poetic voices.[106] Sylvia Plath, through her genius and her struggle, has contributed much to our night vision, and it is tragic that she felt she had to destroy the dependent part of herself rather than help it grow up. Her fate underlines the challenge to women of finding enough support—inner and outer—through love, not approval, to be able to hold the tension between the need for affiliation and the need for creative expression. That, after all, is what we are asking of men.

Suicidal fantasies and attempts plague every profession. Writers have tended to chronicle their suicidal images, making us aware that creativity is no guarantee against death-wishes. Nor can we assume that an audience for self-destructive feelings is a life-support. Death has been portrayed as a seductive Demon Lover throughout history.

Mary Oliver and Marge Piercy have written about the legacy of suicide left them by other writers. Here Piercy exhorts her fellow women writers to resist him:

> He is not pretty, that boy, only well

---

103 Ibid., pp. 239, 215.
104 *My Life a Loaded Gun,* p. 159.
105 Ibid., p. 164.
106 Ibid., pp. 3-4.

advertised. Give your enemies nothing.
Let our tears freeze to stones
we can throw from catapults.
Death is their mercenary, their agent.
He seduces you for hire.
After your death he will pander
your books and explain you.

I know we can't make promises.
Every work pushed out through the jagged
bottleneck sewer of the industry
is a defeat, mutilated before it's born.
My faucets drip at night too. I wake
tired. From the ceiling over my bed
troubles spin down on growing threads.
Only promise if you do get too weary,
take a bank president to lunch,
take a Rockefeller with you. Write
your own epitaph and say it loud.
This life is a war we are not yet
winning for our daughter's children.
Don't do your enemies' work for them.
Finish your own.[107]

In "Members of the Tribe," Mary Oliver refers to suicidal writers who influenced her:

I forgive them
their unhappiness,
I forgive them
for walking out of the world.

But I don't forgive them
for turning their faces away,
for taking off their veils
and dancing for death—

for hurtling
toward oblivion
on the sharp blades
of their exquisite poems, saying:

---

[107] From "Memo," *The Moon Is Always Female,* pp. 86-88.

this is the way.

. . . .

I was, of course, all that time
coming along
behind them, and listening
for advice.

. . . .

And the man who merely
washed Michelangelo's brushes, kneeling
on the damp bricks, staring
every day at the colors pouring out of them,

lived to be a hundred years old.[108]

Adrienne Rich, commenting on the work of Sylvia Plath and Diane Wakoski, finds that in both, "man" appears as a fascination and a terror, qualities found in the relationship to the animus at the stage of mother-domination.

> The charisma of Man seems to come purely from his power over her and his control of the world by force, not from anything fertile or life-giving in him. And in the work of both these poets, it is finally the woman's sense of *herself*—embattled, possessed—that gives the poetry its dynamic charge, its rhythms of struggle, need, will, and female energy. Until recently this female anger and this furious awareness of the Man's power over her were not available materials to the female poet, who tended to write of Love as the source of her suffering, and to view that victimization by Love as an almost inevitable fate.[109]

While the wheels of time move slowly to change outer relationships, women can change their relationship to the inner man. He can be a death-dealing demon or fertile and life-giving.

---

108 *Dream Work,* pp. 32-34.
109 "When We Dead Awaken: Writing as Re-Vision," *On Lies, Secrets, and Silence,* p. 36.

8

In the Mother-World

> Don't think
> because her petal thighs
> leap and her slight
> breasts flatten
> against your chest
> that you warm her
> alligator mind.
> In August
> her hand of snow
> rests on your back.
> Follow her through the mirror.
> My wan sister.
> Love is a trap
> that would tear her
> like a rabbit.
> —Marge Piercy, "Girl in White."

Piercy writes not of the animus himself but of the effect on a woman of having a mother-bound animus. Think of the state of the "spirit," or "mind" or "drive," in the woman pictured here. We get a sense of something weak and colorless. Yet we also sense a great store of hidden energy that may erupt in unusually determined, possibly devious, action . . . like an alligator.

In this "girl" stage of animus development are found mother's daughters, Kores and Persephones, girls of sweet innocence, vulnerable and unpredictable. They lack strong convictions and are, symbolically, ripe for rape. The girl in the poem is "in white," meaning that she is not aware of her shadow and will project it onto others. She is not yet able to step back and look into herself; she sees only her mirror image, distorted by her own unconsciousness.

At this stage a woman may be very intelligent, but her mentality has a passive, unconscious quality, which makes her appear lazy and dumb. She has a cold hand because she is not infused with spirit, which would flesh her out with some fiery warmth. Her inner man, imprisoned in some dark recess of the psyche, only emerges under great pressure. He expresses himself in violent, primitive behavior which she could never acknowledge as her own. The image of the trap is apt; at this stage a woman does feel trapped, regardless of the circumstances.

We have all been there and can regress to this stage under certain circumstances. Young girls normally show a fluctuation in and out of this state as the animus is coming to consciousness. Some women never grow out of it.

The original state of consciousness, barely differentiated from the unconscious, we can only know in glimpses. Though we cannot recall the original experience, even as adults we slip in and out of this state temporarily, in dreams and fantasies, and there are other times when we seek it out. Children take it in degrees; they seem to find comfort in it until adolescence, at which point there is more ambivalence than comfort.

On the most primary level, the symbiotic union of daughter and mother constellates a split from animus energy. This is totally unconscious. The nurturant mother and her child are submerged in the maternal complex. This is not a continual state for the mother—she can move in and out of it to varying degrees—but her daughter is not free as long as her own identity remains unestablished. When animus intrudes on this union—and at this stage he usually appears as a love object in the outer world—it is experienced as a major shock. Because of this, tension is very high in a home with a new baby unless the father has a good relationship with his own feminine side.

The most important part of the father's function in a child's early infancy is to foster the union between mother and child, a task he will enjoy if his feminine side is evolved, or avoid and resent if he is unfulfilled and envious. Indeed, a woman's animus can be said to function like a husband. A strong, loving animus will protect her and her child from harm and intrusions; a weak or childish animus, like a jealous lover, will interfere with the nurturing of her child by demanding attention, calling her away with narcissistic preoccupations.

The positive animus plays an important part in how confidently a

woman proceeds in her feminine tasks. He is like ,
tion for her sense of self-assuredness. Some women
sense and constantly seek reinforcement from outsi
great demands on their husbands, children or society
needs. They cannot tolerate their children acting indep   ... ...
ways that inconvenience them; they are prone to hysterical or oppres-
sive behavior, unconsciously designed to control others.

In a healthy mother-child relationship, movement from the
mother's animus will coincide with the child's need for independence. Then the same process which resulted in giving birth on the
physiological level occurs to effect a psychological separation. The
father also will experience a shift, from protector to severer; his energy can assist the second birth, the psychic separation. Will it be a
gentle midwifing or a violent abandonment?

Being in love, like any strong transference situation, allows us—
or more accurately, compels us—to reexperience the early developmental stages and to project onto the other what we came to expect
from our early and extremely powerful first relationships. If those
early experiences elicited trust, then as adults we approach relationships with benevolent expectations. If the first bonds were weak or
negative, intimacy will be harder to maintain in later life. But there
are exceptions to every psychological rule. In some cases, the powerful urge for self-realization is indomitable.

Symbiotic unions, experienced in adulthood as extreme interdependence, often lead to tensions between friends or lovers. One is
more comfortable being contained than the other, and the movement
outward begins in one before the other is ready. Or we see parents
whose own unsatisfied longing for union arouses fear and ambivalence, so that they vacillate between being nurturant and abusive. The
mother archetype dominates for a while; then the split-off animus energy comes up and dominates ego-consciousness. We have only to
watch ourselves reacting to the alarm clock on a lazy day, or hearing
the telephone ring while enjoying a hot bath, or being interrupted
during lovemaking, to glimpse the energies accompanying the symbiotic stage—that tremendous pull to remain in it, the enormous effort it takes to get out.

In the beginning of ego awareness, although there is some separation from the personal mother, the girl or woman remains fixated in the mother archetype. The masculine is still split off and there is a feeling of alienation toward the animus that expresses itself in fear, indifference or a belittling attitude toward men.

While generally this phase is lived through by about the fourth year of life, women can stay in such a relationship with the unconscious for a lifetime. We can remain fused with mother without appearing to be terribly maladjusted, in a way that men cannot, because so little is expected of women in the outer world, and because so little of what they contribute to the inner world of the family is fully valued and appreciated. The homemaker-mother who receives the appreciation and fidelity of a partner, happy to share his world with her, is less likely to resent her tasks. This is not to say that she will not also want to develop other aspects of herself. It is entirely possible that she will develop her creative powers fully without having to work outside the home.

An undeveloped woman can marry and care for babies without ever leaving her mother's home in her heart and soul. This primitive state of affairs may be reflected in some dysfunction in the family, but she will not be obviously impaired. In contrast, men who do not forge some kind of independence from the mother-world are not easily able to find fulfillment. The modern acceptability of alternative life-styles, such as house-husband or artist supported by others, some homosexual arrangements, communal living, etc., offer some solutions to today's less conventional man.

When contained in the world of mother, women's dreams and fantasies picture the animus as foreign or strange, abusive or abandoning. He may appear as a rapist, a hostile animal or subhuman monster, a dwarf or a gang. In her poem "The Blackstone Rangers," Gwendolyn Brooks describes a gang of young people in their passage through this stage of the mother-world.[110] From the vantage-point of wisdom and compassion, she shows the exquisite poignancy and pain associated with the transition to adulthood.

In mythology this stage is depicted in the story of Demeter and Persephone, where Hades intrudes on the mother-daughter union as

---

[110] *In the Mecca*, pp. 44-48.

rapist and psychopomp, forcing the girl into the underworld. In outer life, mother-bound daughters are extremely vulnerable to the Underground Man, for both are unconscious.

Typical attitudes expressed by women in this stage are: Men are all alike. Men only want one thing. Men can't give love. Men want children, but don't want to take care of them. Who needs men? Men are easy to fool; they like anything false. I can get what I want out of men. I don't have the time (or money, or energy) to read (or exercise, learn, work, help others, enjoy sex, go to a therapist, go to a doctor). My kids (or parents or husband) take up all my time. I'm going home to mother (or to get stoned, or to eat to oblivion, or to die). I can't concentrate enough to . . . I never could . . . I'm just like my mother, she never could . . .

Marge Piercy recreates a situation familiar to most women today: the fickle lover who loves the chase but abandons the loved one when difficulties arise. This is typical of the mother-bound man or woman.

> That sweet sinewy green nymph
> eddying in curves through the grasses:
> she must stop and stare at him.
> Of all the savage secret creatures
> he imagines stealthy in the quivering
> night, she must be made to approach,
> she must be tamed to love him.
> The power of his wanting will turn
> her from hostile dark wandering
> other beyond the circle of his
> campfire into his own, his flesh,
> his other wanting half. To keep her
> she must be filled with his baby,
> weighted down.
> Then suddenly
> the horror of it: he awakens,
> wrapped in the coils of the mother,
> the great old serpent hag,
> the hungry ravening witch who gives
> birth and demands, and the lesser
> mouths of the grinning children

gobbling his substance. He
must cut free.
      An epic battle
in courts and beds and offices,
in barrooms and before the bar
and then free at last, he wanders.
There on the grassy hill, how the body
moves,
    her, the real one,
        green
as a mayfly she hovers and he pounces.[111]

In the fairy tale "Snow White and Rose Red," a mother and her two beautiful daughters, one dark and one light, befriend a wounded bear who takes refuge with them during the winter. Although the circumstances at the opening of the story are of unbalanced male/female energies—there is no masculine presence—the fact that the dark and light are represented by the girls suggests something positive may occur. If the situation were too "white," the outlook would be bleak. Here the feminine trinity of sisters and mother constellates primitive animus energies in the form of a bear and dwarf which must be related to before they can be transformed.

Initially the three women are terrified of the bear, who represents the strong but bewitched masculine. He is potentially a worthy partner, but must be befriended and trusted before his human nature can emerge. The dwarf, as that aspect of the masculine destined to remain mother-bound, is pampered and coddled by the sisters, which makes him even crueler. He remains hostile and ungrateful no matter what they do. He appears to be unredeemable and has to be depotentiated (overcome, incorporated) by the bear.

This is a situation which causes confusion whether dealing with an inner complex or an outer partner. When do we give up and withdraw, and when do we hang in, hoping for relatedness? The fairy tale suggests that a woman must find within herself some positive masculine energy (the bear) to help her overcome the weak, destructive tendencies of the less-developed animus. An example from life

---

[111] "Laocoon Is the Name of the Figure," *Circles on the Water,* p. 290.

would be that a woman calls upon her trust in herself, in her ability to grow, perhaps to follow a treatment program in order to overcome an addiction. As for when to give up on an outer partner, no one other than the woman herself can decide that. It is easy for therapists or friends to see a way out of a relationship that appears to be at an impasse, but until the last shred of hope is lost, people often will not let go.

The domination of the mother archetype precludes any true meeting between man and woman. The failure of the dwarf to relate, in the story above, is a metaphor for the personality characteristic of this stage. The unions such women undertake show certain similar features. Their attachment to the mother or family of origin is a source of enmity between the woman and her partner, the source of mother-in-law jokes as a cultural phenomenon. Or the man may welcome and participate in the symbiosis with mother if he was deprived of it himself. There may be sexual frigidity or lack of interest, overattachment to children, overgeneralizations and opinions about the nature of men without the ability to see an individual man's qualities, or a tendency to use men.

Such women may appear to be natural and spontaneous, with a certain charming lack of self-consciousness. They are appealing to men who are themselves limited to a matriarchal level or see themselves as heroes who can rescue or seduce the woman into being more accessible. The woman may see herself in a victim role in relation to men and may project sadistic fantasies onto them.

Jean Shinoda Bolen describes this character type as a "Persephone woman."[112] This stage can be outgrown if the woman is put into a position where she has to take care of herself. Often such women develop so much charm and are so good at manipulating others that they manage to avoid having to become independent. That is, they find an animus figure who is challenged by their unavailability and will take care of them, usually a man who needs an anima to rescue in the outer world while he avoids his own creative work. Or, as normally happens, individuation proceeds through the upheaval of the state of symbiosis by a movement from the paternal animus.

---

[112] *Goddesses in Everywoman,* pp. 205-215.

Some women stay at this level until their partner becomes ill or dies, or divorces them. Only then do they become aware of their essential separateness.

The animus of women at this stage can be described in the same terms as a mother-dominated male, a classic puer.[113] He lacks stamina. He tends to be lazy and dependent, prone to depression and procrastination. He needs an outside stimulus to get going—a new project or partner, a cause, the excitement of a rebellion or a sexual invitation. He does not have the strength to push through the mother-daughter bond. Rather than working in harmony with the woman's Self and contributing to her survival and well-being, he succumbs to easy pleasure and intoxicants. He may prefer to live in a group situation than alone. He could be a gang member, a terrorist, a chronic prisoner of some kind. Often he is projected onto a married man who can't be faithful but can't leave the marriage. Don Juans, commitment-phobics, pedophiles and those who need a woman as an ornament are all versions of mother-bound men, though often the umbilicus is well disguised.

The woman with such an animus will manifest similar problems, especially when dealing with things of the mind or accomplishments valued by society. She has trouble being committed, or finds herself drawn to men of this type despite her better judgment.

In "Snow White and Rose Red," however, the relationship with the bear is full of possibility. He represents the masculine principle which, though regressed, is available for dialogue. Just as with an actual man, it takes time and work to know whether the inner man is capable of breaking free of the mother complex.

The mother in the fairy tale is not unreasonable, only lacking something. But some women have such a strong and malignant personal mother to contend with that, even with a good deal of animus energy, separation is inordinately difficult. Though they struggle to be independent and even attract relatively strong male partners, they fall again and again into the clutches of the mother through their need for her approval. Jungian analyst Julia McAfee describes such

---

[113] See Marie-Louise von Franz, *Puer Aeternus: A Psychological Study of the Adult Struggle with the Paradise of Childhood.*

women in her exploration of the lives of three women writers, Zelda
Fitzgerald, Anne Sexton and Sylvia Plath.[114] Each lived in the
shadow of a mother whose power-driven animus, finding no creative
outlet in her own life, functioned as a vampire feeding on the creative
energies of her daughter. Two committed suicide, and Zelda died in a
mental hospital fire.[115]

In the following poem, Claudia Lapp describes a dream state in
which the strong masculine energies are present, but something (an
old attitude, belief or stance, held after its time of usefulness?) causes
them to retreat and disappear into the unconscious, leaving her in a
weakened ego-state. It is common to feel the ebb and flow of the
animus energy during biological cycles.

> I'm a horseherder.
> My herd's led by a big bay
> who swims with his ones
> in the wide muddy river.
> On slopes amid evergreens I watch
> black fetlock power in the valley and water.
>
> There's another herder,
> lives in the woods, an old man.
>
> Once upon a time,
> my herd is gone,
> forlock, mane, skin sheen
> last seen churning brown waters.
>
> Have you seen them, old man?
> Nope, no trace of horse,
> just this silly mare
> wiggling her behind and telling jokes.
>
> Soon my mother appears,
> speaking of sickness and journeys.[116]

---

114 "The Cave of the Mirror" (unpublished).

115 It is worth noting that the animus-driven mother is usually the victim
of factors in her life which prevented the development of her own creativity.
On the positive side, without her dedication, her children may not have survived at all, and certainly not as creative, talented women.

116 "Dream Horse Herding," *Cloud Gate,* p. 30.

I want to reiterate that because a work of art reflects a particular stage is no sign that the artist is fixated at that stage. Because of the nature of the ego in the creative process, artists can take us to archaic places they left long ago. A regression to an early state of fusion with the mother is reflected here:

It is a summer evening.
The yellow moths sag
against the locked screens
and the faded curtains
suck over the window sills
and from another building
a goat calls in his dreams.
This is the TV parlour
in the best ward at Bedlam.
The night nurse is passing
out the evening pills.
She walks on two erasers,
padding by us one by one.

My sleeping pill is white.
It is a splendid pearl;
it floats me out of myself,
my stung skin as alien
as a loose bolt of cloth.
I will ignore the bed.
I am linen on a shelf.
Let the others moan in secret;
let each lost butterfly
go home. Old woolen head,
take me like a yellow moth
while the goat calls hush
a-bye.[117]

Often the ocean is the symbol for a return to the imagined peace of the original fusion. In her article entitled "Ocean 1212-W" (her grandmother's phone number at the beach), Sylvia Plath described "the motherly pulse of the sea":

---

[117] Anne Sexton, "Lullabye," in Ellman and O'Clair, *Norton Anthology,* p. 1197.

I sometimes think my vision of the sea is the clearest thing I own. I pick it up, exile that I am, like the purple "lucky stones" I used to collect with a white ring all the way round, or the shell of a blue mussel with its rainbowy angel's fingernail interior; and in one wash of memory the colors deepen and gleam, the early world draws breath.

Breath, that is the first thing. Something is breathing. My own breath? The breath of my mother? No, something else, something larger, farther, more serious, more weary. So behind shut lids I float awhile.[118]

Edna St. Vincent Millay, as one who grew up close to her mother, near the sea, and lived and traveled alone for many years, uses the same self-description in "Exiled":

Searching my heart for its true sorrow,
This is the thing I find to be;
That I am weary of words and people,
Sick of the city, wanting the sea.

Wanting the sticky, salty sweetness
Of the strong wind and shattered spray;
Wanting the loud sound and the soft sound
Of the big surf that breaks all day.[119]

In "The Mirror in Which Two Are Seen As One," Adrienne Rich allows herself to regress to an experience of birth, to be reborn into a spirit different from that of women before her:

Late summer night the insects
fry in the yellowed lightglobe
your skin burns gold in its light
In this mirror, who are you? Dreams of the nunnery
with its discipline, the nursery
with its nurse, the hospital
where all the powerful ones are masked
the graveyard where you sit on the graves
of women who died in childbirth
and women who died at birth

---

[118] *Johnny Panic and the Bible of Dreams,* p. 20.
[119] *Collected Poems,* pp. 105-106.

Dreams of your sister's birth
your mother dying in childbirth over and over
not knowing how to stop
bearing you over and over

your mother dead and you unborn
your two hands grasping your head
drawing it down against the blade of life
your nerves the nerves of a midwife
learning her trade[120]

Rich is here able to imagine giving birth to herself, which requires an advanced capacity for relinquishing conventional comforts. Her ability to reflect on regressive states does not imply lack of ego development, but the talent to articulate for others states which seldom come to consciousness.

Sometimes we see a woman whose ego is well developed but who carries a strong component of the energy of the archetypal mother. Bolen describes this energy in terms of the goddess Demeter.[121] Such a woman will have a preference for the mother-world, but will not necessarily be stuck in it.

Many women have described the feeling-state of mothering and noted how it differs from other states. There is a certain decompression, or divesting of some part of oneself, that is required in making the change from being in the world as a nonmother, and being in the world as a mother. Mothers with careers outside the home feel this process keenly as they switch roles from one situation to the other. There is an attitude one must take on when walking into the home, and leave behind when walking out. Both the taking on and the leaving off require an expenditure of energy that can become very tiring if one has to do it often, regardless of how much one *wants* to do it. This is different from, but related to, the conflict felt by those who must disconnect from children to follow the needs of their inner creativity, a conflict Rich has described so well.

For writing is re-naming. Now, to be maternally with small children all day in the old way, to be with a man in the old way of marriage,

---

[120] *Diving into the Wreck: Poems 1971-1972*, pp. 15-16.
[121] *Goddesses in Everywoman*, pp. 168-196.

requires a holding-back, a putting-aside of that imaginative activity, and demands instead a kind of conservatism. I want to make it clear that I am not saying that in order to write well, or think well, it is necessary to become unavailable to others, or to become a devouring ego. This has been the myth of the masculine artist and thinker; and I do not accept it. But to be a female human being trying to fulfill traditional female functions in a traditional way *is* in direct conflict with the subversive function of the imagination. . . . There must be ways . . . in which the energy of creation and the energy of relation can be united.[122]

Bolen's way of looking at archetypal energy helps explain why some women suffer from this conflict, while others, content solely with the role of mother, or not being one, do not experience the conflict nor the costliness of switching attitudes.

I am not speaking only of the conflict between relation and creation; I am talking about a way of being with children which is different from any other kind of relatedness. Men may feel this as well, though many seem not to, even when caring for children. Women too may not feel it, especially when caring for someone else's children. There is that possibility of fully entering the child's space, attending to the world through the child's body. This is a true mirroring, essential to the well-being of the child's psyche. It requires a giving up of ego-boundaries on the parent's part, a willingness to go back to that original fusion for as long as necessary to fulfill the child's needs. It involves risking being trapped by the child for as long as it needs you, and suffering the rejection when it no longer does.

Being a fully mothering person, and not just a caretaker, *does* require living close to the unconscious, as does being an artist or an analyst. A gentle transition from symbiosis to autonomy occurs when mother and child have a positive relationship to the masculine, to bridge access to the conscious world, as we shall see in the next chapter.

---

[122] "When We Dead Awaken: Writing As Re-Vision," *On Lies, Secrets, and Silence,* p. 43

9

In the Father-World

My candle burns at both ends;
It will not last the night:
But ah, my foes, and oh, my friends—
It gives a lovely light!
—Edna St. Vincent Millay, "First Fig."

Unlike the "Girl in White" of the mother-world, the woman who speaks in this poem is full of spirit, fire and light. This quatrain became the anthem for Millay's generation of social revolution in the 1920s. It captures a spirit of sassy relationship to authority that marks the stage of being in the father-world.

When the bond with the mother-world is penetrated, the intrusion is experienced with great force. The masculine energy, having been split off and withheld in the previous stages, emerges with overpowering impact and captivates the woman or girl, this time into the realm of the Great Father. She experiences a physical and spiritual opening, and responds with the surrender of her total being.

This stage, as described by Neumann, can be compared with Freud's stage of the Electra complex; in Loevinger's model it begins in the Self-Protective and Conformist stages and becomes full-blown in the Self-Aware stage. Freudian theory focuses on the relationships between the instinctual drives in the girl, her mother and father, with an emphasis on sexual energy. Loevinger focuses on the sociopolitical atmosphere, particularly the power of patriarchy and its effect on the family system and the girl's capacity to relate to it as her own agent. Neumann's emphasis is on the archetypal energies unfolding in a preordained order, a universal process that is culture wide, not just a step in reaction to a patriarchal world.

Freud thought that boys and girls both suffered from the events of the phallic stage, where the recognition of the primary sexual relationship between father and mother caused the child to suffer a loss

116

of mother. In boys the loss is experienced with resignation, and with castration anxiety due to being father's rival. At the completion of this stage, the healthy boy will identify with his father; he will relinquish mother and find another woman to replace her. A girl, unable to identify biologically with father, automatically identifies with her first love, mother, while being attracted sexually to father. The experience of being like mother, but physically excited by father, makes her a rival of her own first love and source of identity. Freud believed this experience of betraying mother to be the basis for guilt, shame and penis-envy in women. Like the boy, she has to resign herself to her place in the family in order to find her place in society.

Neumann's model describes similar themes for this stage: in males, the birth of the hero who must overcome the dragon of unconscious dependence, and in females, the invasion of the mother-daughter bond by the energy of the father. There is in both schemas an implication that heterosexuality is expected, which arguably reflects a patriarchal bias. But my understanding is that these stages represent an ideal progression leading to a mature personality free to choose from any number of different lifestyles, including bisexuality and celibacy.

In Loevinger, this stage begins with the girl's recognition of her own individual power and a preoccupation with advantage and control in relationships. Later she will seek approval in groups, and even later will be able to see the relativism of norms and values, but always she is moving toward personal autonomy.

In all three models there is a movement away from fusion with mother, an acceptance of masculine assertiveness and a drive toward independence. Side by side with an experience of loss there is a sense of excitement about something new and promising.

When a woman persists in this stage beyond her early fascination with the personal father, she lives in an attitude of inflation as the special daughter of the archetypal father, unconsciously identified as his partner. There may be a loss of earthiness and an estrangement from the mother-world and from her feminine nature; or, if not an estrangement, a tendency to disparage feminine values except as they are useful to please the father-world.

This stage brings the woman into intellectual and spiritual awareness; if there is a fixation at this stage, we see a puella, hetaira or hysterical personality type—one who depends on the affirmation of a man, rather than her own instincts, for her self-esteem. Ideally, after this stage is resolved, the girl transforms that paternal energy into something more manageable and becomes aware of the full blossoming of her feminine Self. But if this does not happen—through problems with father, his absence or some other disturbance—she can fail to pass through this stage. Being stuck in a positive father complex may lead her to idealize the father-world at the expense of her own creativity; with a negative father complex she may feel continually victimized by a "higher power." Of course, in a society that devalues the feminine a woman is prone to feeling victimized in any case.

We can see the wondrous effects of enthrallment with the father archetype in little girls of two to five years of age, especially when this stage is mirrored by a loving personal father. But even without such mirroring the masculine development in the girl will proceed, modeled on the masculine traits in her mother or others close to her. Diane Wakoski recognized her need for fathering in fantasy and wrote about it in her renowned poem, "The Father of My Country." Here is an excerpt:

> my father
> made me what I am
> a lonely woman
> without a purpose, just as I was
> a lonely child
> without any father. I walked with words, words, and names
> names. Father was not
> one of my words.
> Father was not
> one of my names. But now I say, George you have become my father,
> in his 20th century naval uniform. George Washington, I need your
> love; George, I want to call you Father, Father, my Father,
> Father of my country,
> that is
> me. And I say the name to chant it. To sing it. To lace it around me
> like weaving cloth. Like a happy child on that shining afternoon in
> the palmtree sunset with her mother's trunk yielding treasures,
> I cry and

cry,
Father,
Father,
Father,
have you really come home?[123]

Typical positive effects of this stage are a lifelong spiritedness and the capacity to make decisions. But if the next stage is not accomplished, there are the problems described above.

The life of Edna St. Vincent Millay in many ways exemplifies the advantages and disadvantages of a woman who remains largely within the father-world.

> I, being born a woman and distressed
> By all the needs and notions of my kind,
> Am urged by your propinquity to find
> Your person fair, and feel a certain zest
> To bear your body's weight upon my breast:
> So subtly is the fume of life designed,
> To clarify the pulse and cloud the mind,
> And leave me once again undone, possessed.
> Think not for this, however, the poor treason
> Of my stout blood against my staggering brain,
> I shall remember you with love, or season
> My scorn with pity,—let me make it plain:
> I find this frenzy insufficient reason
> For conversation when we meet again.[124]

This scornful attitude toward lovemaking is a typical stance for Millay. She was a unique and thoroughly creative woman, but the constant presence of a powerful mother and the relative absence of steady fathering appears to have effected a fluctuating sexual identity.

A biography of Millay by Joan Dash reveals that the poet's mother, Cora, was herself abandoned by her mother's early death and had to assume responsibility for five younger siblings.[125] Her strong literary and musical interests were relinquished, but never extinguished, in favor of earning money. She married Henry Millay, a

---

[123] Ellman and O'Clair, *Norton Anthology,* pp. 1351-1354.

[124] *Collected Poems,* sonnet xli, p. 601.

[125] *A Life of One's Own.*

teacher, and had three girls. The eldest was born in 1892, just after Cora's brother had survived injuries suffered in an accident at sea. Because he had received such good treatment at St. Vincent's hospital, Cora gratefully named her baby Edna St.Vincent.

Cora, always a free spirit, refused to accept her husband's gambling with their hard-earned money. We could say that she had a very strong animus. In an action rare for a woman of her position in a small New England town at the turn of the century, she braved public opinion by divorcing Henry and taking charge of her own and her girls' lives alone. In spite of the marital discord, Henry seems to have had a loving relationship with his daughters and a positive effect on them. Millay describes herself at age seven, sadly watching her father walk slowly away across the cranberry patch. Although she would see him again, and even nurse him through illness in her young adulthood, Millay was indelibly affected by this separation.

Cora worked as a nurse, but was determined to create opportunities for her girls to discover and develop their artistic talents. Working at night, she found the energy to sing, play piano, copy music for money, write stories and poetry for periodicals, garden and can foods, bake bread, mend and make clothes. She skimped on necessities in order to buy luxuries, such as concert and theater tickets and magazines. The three sisters wrote and performed their own plays and songs, and roamed freely about the New England seacoast. By the time Edna was twelve, Cora was spending several days or weeks at a time away as a live-in nurse, leaving her in charge.

The bohemian style of their household, with its emphasis on cultivation of the intellect and the arts, was due to Cora's influence and energy; it prepared Edna for life in Greenwich Village in the early 1900s among the artists and writers who found a haven there. Cora's wit, mastery of the art of argument, double entendre and repartee, also helped Edna with the skills she would use as the first woman recipient of a Pulitzer prize for poetry. She won it for "Ballad of the Harp-Weaver," a poem about the devotion of a mother who, by sheer will and spirit, saves her child from freezing to death. It can be seen as a metaphor for the sacrifices required to keep alive the creative Divine Child.

Because independence and ambition in those days were considered the province of men, and also because Cora had wanted a son, Edna, who adored her mother, seems to have taken on a male identity, even calling herself "Vincent." She seemed to care little for the conventional womanly virtues of passivity and tenderness. Though petite and frail looking, she was fiercely headstrong and achievement oriented. Without a father to contest the male role, Edna appears to have remained in some sort of boyish identity with her mother for the remainder of their lives. Her letters reveal her longing for the safety of the little family-band, her use of babytalk when addressing her mother and sisters, her clinging to herself as an extension of Cora long after it had become damaging to her adult status. She showed no interest in establishing her own family.

Because of their poverty, Millay did not consider college, but at age seventeen she published "Renascence," a poem which won so much acclaim that she was encouraged to go to Vassar. Cora distrusted college, afraid that it robbed one of genius and originality, but Millay seems to have been in no such danger. In college she was seen as eccentric and brilliant; she excelled as an actress, scholar, playwright, singer and composer. Five feet tall, often described as elfin, with tiny bone structure and bright red hair, she was also resented by some for her high-handedness, inconsiderateness, temperamental bossiness and a tendency to withdraw when bored.

After graduating she moved to Greenwich Village and brought her family to live with her as soon as she could. She espoused a strong feminist attitude toward marriage, as confining women to the roles of cook and baby-tender, and turned down proposals from several ardent lovers. Her love affairs always followed the same pattern—a quickly passionate beginning, a period of idyllic companionship, then bickering and discord, the frantic fear of being held down, and finally her abandonment of the relationship. In an environment where other women married and continued to pursue their own development as artists, she contrived to maintain her separateness, perhaps to cope with her fear of losing her identity as "Vincent," the mother's boy.

One of her lovers, the writer Edmund Wilson, felt that withdrawal was her natural condition. He pointed out the central theme of claustrophobia in her poem "Renascence" and throughout her work. While the poem is loved for its affirmation of the human spirit, it is possible to see it also as a reflection of her phobia.[126] Dash writes:

> She is afraid of being buried alive, that is, of staying home, shel-
> tered, enclosed, protected by her mother as she is sheltered and en-
> closed, first by the hills and woods, and later by the grave itself. But
> what she most deeply fears she also most deeply desires, for such is
> the nature of claustrophobia, as of any phobia. Childhood and mater-
> nal protection are what she most desperately craves—yet if she per-
> mits herself to imagine them she realizes they will crush her and cut
> her off forever from God's sweet world. . . . In reality, the immediate
> effect of "Renascence" was as liberating as the final stanza of the
> poem itself, since it brought the small-town girl to the attention of
> the world.[127]

Millay, confronted by friends and lovers with her fear of and rebellion against womanliness, would not submit, neither to the confines of marriage and motherhood nor to psychoanalysis which had
become popular. Perhaps she could not face the reality that loving
and committing oneself to one man meant the possibility of separation and loss, such as she had suffered with her father. She illustrates the incomplete process of the stage of self-surrender to the paternal archetype. In accepting her mother's animus drives, she sub-
mitted to the masculine ideal of accomplishment and recognition, but
the process was never completely worked through in terms of the father's penetration of the mother-daughter bond.

For many years she turned down suitors and corresponded with
the dashing Arthur Ficke, who kept himself always a little beyond
her reach; such is the typical romance sustained by the woman (or
man) who fears intimacy. But after years of travel, both alone and
with her mother, exhausted by poverty and recurring illnesses, she
met an unusual man at exactly the optimum moment.

Eugen Jan Boissevain, descendant of generations of international
banker-journalist-adventurers, was a businessman, playboy, devotee
of culture. A widower who had nursed one strong woman, a suf-
fragette lawyer, before her untimely demise, he was immediately
drawn to Edna when he met her seven years after his wife's death.

---

[126] Ibid., p. 129.
[127] Ibid.

Edna was fragile and shy, but talented and famous; Eugen was confident and popular with men and women, for he had well-developed masculine and feminine personality traits. He took Edna to his refuge and tended her like a mother until she recovered her health. He was content to see himself as her guardian and interface with the world. He managed her business engagements as well as their social life, their home and staff of servants, leaving Edna free to write. This became their lifestyle until his death at about age seventy. It is believed that Eugen did not expect fidelity from her, but little is actually known about her lovelife after their marriage.

It is known that it was not always an idyllic union. Edna was given to temper outbursts, which Eugen took in stride. He seems to have fostered a childish quality in her, which had its dark side, eventually showing up in their abuse of alcohol and an atmosphere of hypochondria which marked most of Edna's life. Ironically, the dependent cloistered life she had always dreaded and rebelled against became her lot at Steepletop, their spacious isolated estate.

But the marriage lasted and she remained a poet. After Eugen's death she stayed at home, reclusive and phoneless, with only one helper who looked in on her daily until she died of a heart attack at age fifty-eight, not long after her husband-parent. Although her poetry lost popularity with the times, especially after the arrival of T.S. Eliot on the literary scene and the advent of a more intellectual and austere style of poetry, she continued to be productive and the gift to which she and Eugen had dedicated their lives was preserved.

Millay's life, rich and full of creative energy, was clearly bound by the father-world. Picturing her in the earliest years, stimulated by devoted parents who both valued learning, we see why. It would be misleading to imply that being infused with father-energy is a rare experience, or that this, and other shifts in the psyche, occur only once in a lifetime. It is more accurate to think of these movements of psychic energies in terms of a spiral. We seem to repeat some experiences over and over, each time integrating them from a different vantagepoint; each time, if there is awareness and a strong ego, a little more differentiation occurs.

The "father's daughter" has an animus that is concerned with power and is extremely judgmental; consequently she may be a perfectionist with respect to herself and others. It may be difficult for her to express her criticisms openly, but, unless she finds a constructive outlet for her perfectionism, it infects her and influences her relationships by injecting an atmosphere of suppressed contempt.

The woman in this stage often has an eating disorder. Control is an important issue, as is being right; it is difficult to admit mistakes because the inner judge is so unforgiving and humiliating. At the same time, this powerful animus brings with him a lot of excitement. A woman, projecting onto an outer man her own powerful spirit, can tolerate his sadistic treatment because life seems so insipid and dull without him. She enjoys being adoring and suppliant. She sings the blues and loves it, as long as a man is around to take the projection. Alone, she must suffer from the internal perfectionist, with feelings of inferiority and depression. As one woman told me regarding her father, "I was always tapdancing for him. But I found myself having to tapdance faster and faster, until I was exhausted."

Typical of this developmental stage are the many versions of the Pygmalion story, in which a male creator fashions a woman to his idealistic standards of perfection. In "The Phantom of the Opera," a woman is vulnerable to the seduction of the Phantom, her musical mentor, because of her desire to please her real father who has died. Bound to her father by death, she projects his spirit onto the adoring but power-driven Phantom.

The dynamics of the Phantom are interesting in themselves. Because of his narcissistic wound, a facial deformity, he cannot "face" the rejection that exposing his loving side would bring, and so he resorts to power as a compensation. This is generally true of narcissistic persons; they use power to compensate for the fear and loneliness of their own inner child, of whom too much was expected. Defending against memories of their own buried, imperfect child, they demand nothing short of everything from the outer child. We can see this kind of animus operating throughout Millay's life. The little girl, afraid of being in charge without her mother around to comfort her, compensates by adopting a masculine stance. She enjoys her power over men, but cannot risk the sexual and psychological surrender that would leave her vulnerable to another separation.

A memory from childhood emerges: seeing myself being in-structed to recite this poem at age three, or thereabouts:

> Ribbons at my fingers
> Roses at my feet
> I'm my Daddy's darling . . .
> Don't you think I'm sweet?

As the poem implies, little girls at this stage focus on themselves as a reflection of father. This only becomes unhealthy when it is the basis for relationships in adult life. Darling and her Daddy—or some other father figure—are not truly related, but somehow play off each other, delighting in the impression each are making. The adored man, if he is narcissistic, will use the woman or his daughter for his own ends without considering what is good for her.

In therapy women describe terrible injustices suffered for the sake of father's or mother's reputation. What the neighbors might think is more important than the well-being of the child. Often it is the mother, herself a father's daughter, who conveys the inordinate con-cern for appearances in order to gain power in the community. Lying to maintain appearances is often part of the picture. Several women have told me about becoming pregnant as adolescents and having to submit to an abortion at the insistence of their parents. A particularly evil development is when parents deny it ever happened and maintain the fiction that the daughter had never been pregnant at all. It takes courage to relive this kind of nightmarish experience, to assimilate the pain and recover part of oneself that dies with the baby.

How do we relate this stage of father-worship to religious experi-ence? On this issue schools of psychology are divided. Jungian thought conceives of the ever-present archetypal energies as always available for appropriate expression. This is not simply sublimation, but a calling up of the eternal energies in their time. It is appropriate to be immersed in the archetypal experiences of mothering and father-ing when one is a parent. It is also appropriate to be immersed in these energies when we are relating to the Divine, which evokes re-sponses on all levels of our being. Spiritual energy is not confined to one's personal history, nor is it an aberration, a leftover from a pre-vious stage. Although religious feelings are strongly elicited and vul-nerable to damage at this stage, they are not "nothing but" a byprod-

uct of father-worship, but an attitude available at any age in response
to the recognition of our relatively unknowable place in the universe.

"Engagement" is a meditation of Teresa of Avila, whose surrender
to God took her to many levels of relatedness with the Divine. This
prayer seems to me to illustrate the state of surrender of the woman
to the good Father-God as His loving spouse-daughter.

> Here below when two people are engaged,
> there is discussion about
> whether they are alike,
> whether they love each other, and
> whether they might meet together
> so as to become more satisfied with each other.
>
> So, too, in the case of this union with God,
> the agreement has been made,
> and this soul is well informed about
> the goodness of her Spouse
> and determined to do God's will in everything
> and in as many ways as she sees might make
> God happy.
>
> And God,
> as one who understands clearly
> whether these things about the betrothed are so,
> is happy with her.
>
> As a result God grants the mercy,
> for God desired her to know Him more
> and that they might meet together,
> as they say,
> and be united.[128]

When this stage is not received by a loving father and the child
feels spurned or abandoned to carry this powerful archetypal energy
alone, the negative effects are also usually lifelong. The dark father
functions more like a Trickster or Magician than a loving God, as in
this poem by Sylvia Plath:

> I shall never get you put together entirely,

---

[128] *Meditations with Teresa of Avila,* p. 75.

Pieced, glued, and properly jointed.
Mule-bray, pig-grunt, and bawdy cackles
Proceed from your great lips.
It's worse than a barnyard.

Perhaps you consider yourself an oracle,
Mouthpiece of the dead, or of some god or other.
Thirty years now I have laboured
To dredge the silt from your throat.
I am none the wiser.

Scaling little ladders with gluepots and pails of lysol
I crawl like an ant in mourning
Over the weedy acres of your brow
To mend the immense skull-plates and clear
The bald, white tumuli of your eyes.

A blue sky out of the Oresteia
Arches above us. O father, all by yourself
You are pithy and historical as the Roman Forum.
I open my lunch on a hill of black cypress.
Your fluted bones and acanthine hair are littered

In their old anarchy to the horizon-line.
It would take more than a lightning-stroke
To create such a ruin.
Nights, I squat in the cornucopia
Of your left ear, out of the wind,

Counting the red stars and those of plum-colour.
The sun rises under the pillar of your tongue.
My hours are married to shadow.
No longer do I listen for the scrape of a keel
On the blank stones of the landing.[129]

Plath wrote an even more scathing account of her relationship with
her personal father. "Daddy" has become a classic in the literature of
modern women, perhaps because so many have suffered at the hands
of abusive fathers. Here is the last verse:

There's a stake in your fat black heart
And the villagers never liked you.

---

[129] "The Colossus," in Ellman and O'Clair, *Norton Anthology,* p. 1294.

They are dancing and stamping on you.
They always *knew* it was you.
Daddy, daddy, you bastard, I'm through.[130]

In the following poem Mary Oliver also conveys her suffering at the failure of the father to nurture, but experiences a redemption of forgiveness. This is typical of women who pass successfully through the father-world. They are able to incorporate mercy and compassion into their need for perfection; however, this requires a willingness to deal with the resentment and rage that precede true forgiveness.

My father, for example,
who was young once
and blue-eyed,
returns
on the darkest of nights
to the porch and knocks
wildly at the door,
and if I answer I
 must be prepared
for his waxy face,
for his lower lip
swollen with bitterness.
And so, for a long time,
I did not answer,
but slept fitfully
between his hours of rapping.
But finally there came the night
when I rose out of my sheets
and stumbled down the hall.
The door fell open

and I knew I was saved
and could bear him,
pathetic and hollow,
with even the least of his dreams
frozen inside him,
and the meanness gone.
And I greeted him and asked him

---

[130] *Ariel,* pp. 49-51.

into the house,
and lit the lamp,
and looked into his blank eyes
in which at last
I saw what a child must love,
I saw what love might have done
had we loved in time.[131]

Another image of the "visitor" is as a seductive, powerful authority figure to whom one must surrender:

Everything's just as it was: fine hard snow
beats against the dining room windows,
and I myself have not changed:
even so, a man came to call.

I asked him:" What do you want?"
He said, "To be with you in hell."
I laughed: "It seems you see
plenty of trouble ahead for us both."

But lifting his dry hand
he lightly touched the flowers.
"Tell me how they kiss you,
tell me how you kiss."

And his half-closed eyes
remained on my ring.
Not even the smallest muscle moved
in his serenely angry face.
Oh, I know it fills him with joy—
this hard and passionate certainty
that there is nothing he needs,
and nothing I can keep from him.[132]

A similar aura of irresistible horror lurks forever in the mind of every incest victim. The archetypal power of the father is what makes a girl's experience of incest so damaging, unmanageable and enduring. Indeed, the father archetype colors virtually every seduction of a woman by an authority figure—attorney, professor, employer, pas-

---

[131] "A Visitor," *Dream Work*, pp. 40-41.
[132] Anna Akhmatova, "The Guest," *Twenty Poems*, p. 15.

tor, physician, group leader, therapist. Even if the interaction is loving and not abusive, the inequality of such relationships automatically constellates the powerful energy of the father archetype and can create a larger-than-life wound in the woman.

Ultimately, the perpetrator of incest is also marked, by having to carry forever, at least unconsciously, responsibility for the misuse of power. Mary Oliver conveys this in chilling images:

> You are the dark song
> of the morning;
> serious and slow,
> you shave, you dress,
> you descend the stairs
> in your public clothes
> and drive away, you become
> the wise and powerful one
> who makes all the days
> possible in the world.
> But you were also the red song
> in the night,
> stumbling through the house
> to the child's bed,
> to the damp rose of her body,
> leaving your bitter taste.
> And forever those nights snarl
> the delicate machinery of the days.
> When the child's mother smiles
> you see on her cheekbones
> a truth you will never confess;
> and you see how the child grows—
> timidly, crouching in corners.
> Sometimes in the wide night
> you hear the most mournful cry,
> a ravished and terrible moment.
> In your dreams she's a tree
> that will never come to leaf—
> in your dreams she's a watch
> you dropped on the dark stones
> till no one could gather the fragments—
> in your dreams you have sullied and murdered,

and dreams do not lie.[133]

Perhaps no one has written more passionately about the effect of patriarchal fathers and patriarchal society on the lives of women than Adrienne Rich. She describes her relationship to her father:

> For about twenty years I wrote for a particular man, who criticized and praised me and made me feel I was indeed "special." The obverse side of this, of course, was that I tried for a long time to please him, or rather, not to displease him. And then of course there were other men—writers, teachers—the Man, who was not a terror or a dream but a literary master and a master in other ways less easy to acknowledge. And there were all those poems about women, written by men: it seemed to be a given that men wrote poems and women frequently inhabited them. These women were almost always beautiful, but threatened with the loss of beauty, the loss of youth—the fate worse than death.[134]

Here she speaks of the "drudging child," captive to father's perfectionism, who becomes a "woman with a mission":

> The faithful drudging child
> the child at the oak desk whose penmanship,
> hard work, style will win her prizes
> becomes the woman with a mission, not to win prizes
> but to change the laws of history.
> How she gets this mission
> is not clear, how the boundaries of perfection
> explode, leaving her cheekbone grey with smoke
> a piece of her hair singed off, her shirt
> spattered with earth . . . Say that she grew up in a house
> with talk of books, ideal societies—
> she is gripped by a blue, a foreign air,
> a desert absolute: dragged by the roots of her own will
> into another scene of choices.[135]

Indeed, the woman with a mission is typically a father's daughter.

---

[133] "Rage," *Dream Work*, p. 12.

[134] "When We Dead Awaken: Writing As Re-Vision," *On Lies, Secrets, and Silence*, pp. 38-39.

[135] *Sources*, p. 30.

Hillman describes this type as "soul and spirit confounded."[136] One woman told me the only way she could satisfy the nagging father in her head was to write. As soon as she finished one project, she barely had time to relax before she was compelled to begin another. In this prose-poem, Adrienne Rich speaks directly to the patriarch, now from a position of distance and objectivity born of honest inner work:

> For years I struggled with you: your categories, your theories, your will, the cruelty which came inextricable from your love. For years all arguments I carried on in my head were with you. I saw myself, the eldest daughter raised as a son, taught to study but not to pray, taught to hold reading and writing sacred: the eldest daughter in a house with no son, she who must overthrow the father, take what he taught her and use it against him.
>
> After your death I met you again as the face of patriarchy, could name at last precisely the principle you embodied, there was an ideology at last which let me dispose of you, identify the suffering you caused, hate you righteously as part of a system, the kingdom of the fathers. I saw the power and arrogance of the male as your true watermark; I did not see beneath it the suffering of the Jew, the alien stamp you bore, because you had deliberately arranged that it should be invisible to me. It is only now, under a powerful, womanly lens, that I can decipher your suffering and deny no part of my own.[137]

In contrast, Glenda Taylor captures the ecstatic quality of the invasion of the paternal uroboros, which in the adult woman is experienced as a transcendent experience of the Divine:

> A quote from the conversations of a 19th century Bengalese spiritual master Ramakrishna —"One day it was suddenly revealed to me that everything is Pure Spirit. The utensils of worship, the altar, the doorframe—all Pure Spirit. Men, animals, and other living beings— all Pure Spirit. Then, like a madman, I began to shower flowers in all directions. Whatever I saw, I worshipped."
>
> Likewise,
> one day,

---

[136] *Anima,* p. 77.
[137] *Sources,* p. 15.

I too
saw you
as Pure Spirit
and showered my flowers
of worshipful devotion
like a madman,
unsolicited and inexplicably.

     laughing,
     chanting,
     dancing,
     weeping for the joy of it,
I flung my song of celebration
at you and over you and around you,
drowning in petals,

     some pale, fragile, transparent,
     others radiant, impassioned,
     apparently personal, sensual,
     unquestionably erotic,
astounding you, no doubt,
to see me thus
orgiastically transfixed,
and sending you
in search of safety,

     desperately seeking
     some psychic umbrella
     to shield yourself
     from my flowering shower
     of ecstasy.
You were right,
perhaps,
to hide;
energy thus unleashed
obliterates boundaries
and All sees itself as One;
yours and mine become
that-of-the-Universe,
property lines indefensible
and unknown.

But Ramakrishna and I
do not relent:

You (along with All Else)
ARE
Pure Spirit,
Holiness and Wholeness and
Being Incarnate,
and I worship you
with or without consent,
unceasingly,
ecstatically,
    (otherwise,
      I am given to know,
      lest someone dance this Seeing dance,
      you and I and the universe,
      all stars and trees and centipedes,
      would, instantly,
      cease to
      be.)

So, be forewarned.
Take care and cover,
for at any time,
my mad one's dance
may circle back to You,
and another rain of petals
of perfect adoration
and intense devotion
fully flowered,
may descend.

Then, can you,
will you, then,
be free, and,
(oh, let it be)
laugh,
ecstatically,
back at me?[138]

    Caught up in the power of an archetypal energy, we cannot understand why everyone else does not feel the same. Thus the woman

---

[138] "Yes, Yes, Ramakrishna," *Life Is a River,* pp. 61-63.

in thrall to her father-energy often finds herself alienated from others, particularly men, who tend to be threatened by its intensity. The poet H.D. has the high priestess of Zeus speak:

> Here am I, your daughter,
> Zeus, provider,
> I bring millet in a basket,
> white-grain;
>
> I am late
> but come again,
> after long absence;
>
> I have lain
> with strange lovers;
>
> each one was your
> power and steadiness
> that grew luminous;
>
> trust that failed
> was forgotten,
>
> evil has no part
> in the white-lily,
> set in marble whorls
> upon your altar;
>
> what lily unfurls
> regardless of your light?
>
> to what child
> are you pitiless?[139]

   In the next stage, the experience of a more contemporary-feeling animus energy displaces the powerful father. Like Dorothy's Wizard of Oz, the father complex loses its power and something else within becomes more sturdy and sure.

---

[139] From "Dodona," *H.D.: Collected Poems, 1912-1944,* pp. 408-409.

10
Brother, Hero
and Patriarchal Partner

At the top of the great oak
As I said your name,
We saw him. He was there. He spoke.
The bird of flame.

—May Sarton, from "The Oriole."

Freed from total immersion in the world of the mother by an infusion of spiritual energy from the father archetype, the girl experiences certain masculine qualities which she cannot express directly. To the extent that she perceives these qualities but refuses to identify them as her own, she will project them onto another.

First the father figure is the recipient of these projections. He may remain so throughout her life, which will be a life of dedication to the empowerment of the patriarchy, either through her worshipfulness or her rebelliousness. Usually, however, she will outgrow enthrallment to the father-world and begin to look to males of her own age group with whom to ally herself. This may be a big brother type of relationship, or a hero or anti-hero idealization; in any case, it is someone she can admire, one who reflects her "otherness," while she can continue to identify with the feminine ego-state.

In a patriarchal society this usually means she will assume a subordinate role and will give up some of her authority to the object of her projections. Today's young women are not limited to such relationships before developing their own authority. But whether or not she allows males the dominant role, there is the attraction of the other to be explored.

The following two poems explore vastly different images of male otherness. In "Orion," Mary Oliver portrays the constellation of the huntsman as her companion and teacher:

I love Orion, his fiery body, his ten stars,
his flaring points of reference, his shining dogs.
"It is winter," he says.
"We must eat," he says. Our gloomy
and passionate teacher.
                    Miles below
in the cold woods, with the mouse and the owl,
with the clearness of water sheeted and hidden,
with the reason for the wind forever a secret,
he descends and sits with me, his voice
like the snapping of bones.
                    Behind him
everything is so black and unclassical; behind him
I don't know anything, not even
my own mind.[140]

Imaging much greater tension between the sexes, Millay describes
a scene between an earthbound hunter and a young woman who
hopes to distract him with love:

"Huntsman, what quarry
On the dry hill
Do your hounds harry?
When the red oak is bare
And the white oak still
Rattles its leaves
In the cold air:
What fox runs there?"

"Girl, gathering acorns
In the cold autumn,
I hunt the hot pads
That ever run before,
I hunt the pointed mask
That makes no reply,
I hunt the red brush
Of remembered joy."

"To tame or to destroy?"
"To destroy."

---

[140] *Dream Work,* p. 49.

"Huntsman, hard by
In a wood of grey beeches
Whose leaves are on the ground,
Is a house with a fire;
You can see the smoke from here.
There's supper and a soft bed
And not a soul around.
Come with me there;
Bide there with me;
And let the fox run free."

The horse that he rode on
Reached down its neck,
Blew upon her acorns,
Nuzzled them aside;
The sun was near setting;
He thought," Shall I heed her?"
He thought," Shall I take her
For a one-night's bride?"

He smelled the sweet smoke,
He looked the lady over;
Her hand was on his knee;
But like a flame from cover
The red fox broke—
And "Hoick! Hoick!" cried he.[141]

The Orion of Adrienne Rich carries a very different quality from Oliver's. Although as an inspiring brother he symbolized her creativity, she is disillusioned:

Far back when I went zig-zagging
through tamarack pastures
you were my genius, you
. . . .
my fierce half-brother, staring
down from that simplified west . . .

She tells him about her sense of failure as a wife and mother, but gets no comfort from him:

---

[141] *Collected Poems*, pp. 332-334.

Pity is not your forte.
Calmly you ache up there
pinned aloft in your crow's nest,
my speechless pirate! . . .[142]

Many women gradually develop qualities of the masculine archetype through a sisterly or buddy-type relationship with men, a stage preceding the sudden intrusion of the hero, which is felt with all the romantic power of the previous intrusion of the father. A loving connection with the brother often makes way for this next phase and prepares the female ego for the energy of the hero/heroine.[143]

The heroic attitude seems to be actualized in several ways: one is an awareness of one's philosophical mind and the capacity to think for oneself, attended by a feeling of righteousness and authority. This indicates the beginning of the introjection of the patriarch which was previously projected. The second heroic attitude involves the recognition and acceptance of one's sexuality. A later development of the heroic attitude is the recognition and appreciation of one's yin-ego, which values being as well as doing. The female is coming to know her own mind, her own body and her own feminine attitudes.

While typically the heroic stage occurs in early adolescence, it may arrive later in life. Jung's concept of the animus as interface between ego and Self becomes more apparent here. The presence of the animus can help with the differentiation that makes possible the choice of trusting the feminine Self and identifying herself, again, as a feminine person, this time with a degree of sexual awareness which was not present in childhood.

Trust is an essential element in the feminine association of courage with endurance and survival, as much as brave action. As with all changes in consciousness, there is ambivalence in leaving the world of the father and entering the heroic position. The fundamental heroic task is to acquire courage and overcome fear. Here the fear involves thinking and feeling independently. The girl who has had a positive experience of father will move to this stage with minimal fear.

---

[142] From "Orion," *Leaflets: Poems 1965-1968*, pp. 11-12.

[143] I find it helpful to use the images of Coline Covington ("In Search of the Heroine") with the hero and heroine counterbalancing one another in an ongoing process of separation/deintegration and dependency/reintegration.

Sometimes there is anger when the woman becomes aware of the illusions she has maintained in idealizing the father or the patriarchy. Here Marge Piercy condemns the death-dealing aspects of the senex:

> In the house of power grown old but unyielding
> the emperor sits severe in mail, watching all that creep;
> even over the grasshoppers and the minnows, over the leaves
> that catch sun into food, he wields barrenness.
> He holds a globe like something he might bite into
> and an ankh, for he will carry his dominion into the living cells
> and the ancient cabala of the genes he plans to revise
> till everything born is programmed to obey.
> The Man from Mars with sterile mountains at his back—
> perhaps strip-mined, perhaps the site of weapons testing—
> if we opened that armor like a can, would we find a robot?
> quaking old flesh? the ghost of an inflated bond issue?
>
> Evil old men banal as door knobs
> who rule the world like a comic strip,
> you are the Father Who Eats His Young.
> Power abhors a vacuum, you say and sit down at the Wurlitzer
> to play the color organ of poison gases.
> All roads lead to the top of the pyramid on the dollar bill
> where hearts are torn out and skulls split to feed
> the ultimate ejaculating machine, the ruling class climax by missile.
> The gnats of intelligence who have bugged every pay toilet
> in the country sing in your beard of court cases and jails to come.
> It is reason enough to bomb a village if it cannot be bought.
> Heavy as dinosaurs, plated and armored,
> you crush the land under your feet and flatten it.
> Lakes of smoking asphalt spread where your feet have trod.
>
> You exiled the Female into blacks and women and colonies.
> You became the armed brain and the barbed penis and the club.
> You invented agribusiness, leaching the soil to dust,
> and pissed mercury in the rivers and shat slag on the plains,
> withered your emotions to ulcers,
> strait-jacketed the mysteries and sent them to shock therapy.
> Your empress is a new-model car with breasts.
>
> There is in the dance of all things together no profit
> for each feeds the next and all pass through each other,

the serpent whose tail is in her mouth,
our mother earth turning.
Now the wheel of the seasons sticks and the circle is broken
and life spills out in an oil slick to rot the seas.
You are the God of the Puritans playing war games on computers:
you can give birth to nothing
except death.[144]

Other feelings of women at this stage include pride and fear
around the mystery of menstrual blood and the biological rhythms
over which we have no conscious control. There is sadness in many
women over the loss of innocence, particularly in the acceptance of
sexual feelings as their own and not just a reaction to something done
to them. Many women tell me of the sadness they felt when they first
realized they had to relinquish their tomboy or buddy relationships
and acquire the sexual differentiation which would thrust them into
another stage of development. Freud attributed these feelings to penis
envy, but as we have seen, most psychologists recognize that as an
oversimplification of a highly complicated set of experiences.

Now the mother-daughter relationship becomes incredibly complex, as the feminine ego must mediate loyalty, love and identification as a potential mother, as well as rivalry and separateness often
accompanied by shame and guilt. This rivalry, experienced first at
the phallic stage, is now sexualized and intensified with adolescent
hormonal impetus.

At the same time there is great excitement as energy flows from
the feminine Self and the animus, with the need to be seen as different from men. In adolescence all the narcissistic pleasures are reca-
pitulated, with their consequent swings between elation and despair.
It is not surprising that, in the absence of rituals to contain these con-
tradictory energies, many girls resolve the tension by getting pregnant, unconsciously choosing their own initiation process.

In my own life, my brother entered puberty first, leaving me behind to grapple with feelings of closeness, loss and strange stirrings
of the mind. The following excerpt from a long poem reflects this period, especially my concern with time and the relationship between
cyclical and linear time that was dawning on me then:

---

[144] "The Emperor," *Circles on the Water,* pp. 133-134.

He stares into the mirror, thinking of today;
"Don't you think I'm handsome?" I say, "Yes,"
but can't express how thinking of forever
both sharpens and clouds my sight.
He tries on looks as I would dresses,
and satisfied, goes dancing, thinking of tonight.

That poem and the one that follows by Madeline Tiger both call up the nostalgic atmosphere of entering puberty, along with the glimpses of the philosophic mind which appears at that time. "Older Brothers . . ."

walk
like storks
stalk territory
crane toward
corners
of sky not to
ask why they're
here, not elsewhere,
wary of the question-
answer trap, the snap
verdict; but they are
addicted to
grouping; ergo, their
cliques and slick talk
between the long legs of
their secrets and loves. Still
brothers who may be
taller walk near
the others, hear
awes, gripes, fear, peer-
group peckings, pick
what they don't know
they need to hold
themselves somehow
dear, all the more-
so dear. It is said
the older ones are their own
arbiters, unduly
arrogant, derogatory;

they are marked and re-
marked unique in this
they bask: It is the next best
state to being blessed
as the darlings
once they might have been
before they got so grown
out of the now too easy
brother/sister/hood
of jangling younger siblings and until
they get grown gracefully
up.
Older brothers skulk in corners
waiting for the past
to catch up with their long legs.

Would you be shocked if
they broke out
with lovesongs?

Brothers and fathers are often embarrassed and confused by their sexual reactions to the girl at this stage, and she is usually unconscious of her seductiveness. They, particularly fathers, may withdraw their affection in ways that feel abrupt and rejecting to the daughter. This delicate time is extremely important in determining the woman's self-esteem. Naturally an identification with the powerful archetypal feminine is crucial, and "good-enough" mothering must be available. It is also a time when the adult males in her life need to feel confident in their own identity and impulse control, in order to be appreciative of the budding woman without being perceived as seductive, invasive of her privacy or rejecting.

While the brother-relationship can open the way during this period of transition, fixation is also a possibility. The movement to the heroic animus carries anxieties which can be avoided by remaining emotionally tied to the brother. A patient's brother experienced labor pains when she did.[145]

---

[145] See Linda Leonard, *On the Way to the Wedding,* chapter 3, for discussion of problems developing in siblings whose attachment is too fixated; also Nor Hall, *The Moon and the Virgin,* pp. 127-132.

At this stage the attitudes associated with Artemis, the huntress whose only male love is her twin, Apollo, vie with those of Aphrodite, goddess of love and transformation. My bias is to recommend supporting Artemis in preadolescence. There are many pressures on children to become sexually enlightened before they are biologically and psychologically ready. The transition may be easier taken slowly. The enchanted world of the prepubescent whose attention is captured by the wonders of science and nature, participation in sports, caring for animals and smaller children, arts and crafts and domestic skills, will soon enough be invaded by powerful sexual energies. In our anxiety about our own sexuality and the competition for partners, we sometimes concentrate on preparing our children for sexual relatedness before they are ready to give up their hermaphroditic qualities. Millay's poem, "Daphne," pictures a girl in transition, sexually aware and taunting:

> Why do you follow me?—
> Any moment I can be
> Nothing but a laurel-tree.
>
> Any moment of the chase
> I can leave you in my place
> A pink bough for your embrace.
>
> Yet if over hill and hollow
> Still it is your will to follow,
> I am off:—to heel, Apollo! [146]

The acceptance of the male partner as a sexual being marks a powerful change in attitude. The acceptance of the inner sexual partner means the claiming of her own sexuality, and the acceptance of an outer partner means risking exposure of her sexual vulnerability. At this point there is little fear of loss of boundaries, for there is not so strong a sense of self. Later, though, when a woman has had some experience of losing herself in relationships, even more frightening than the sexual vulnerability is the risk of losing one's boundaries, as this poem by Josephine Miles describes:

---

[146] *Collected Poems,* p. 141.

As difference blends into identity
Or blurs into obliteration, we give
To zero our position at the center,
Withdraw our belief and baggage.

As rhyme at the walls lapses, at frontiers
Customs scatter like a flight of snow
And boundaries moonlike draw us out, our opponents
Join us, we are their refuge.

As barriers between us melt, I may treat you
Unkindly as myself, I may forget
Your name as my own. Then enters
Our anonymous assailant.

As assonance by impulse burgeons
And that quaver shakes us by which we are spent,
We may move to consume another with us,
Stir into parity another's cyphers.

Then when our sniper steps to a window
In the brain, starts shooting, and we fall surprised,
Of what we know not do we seek forgiveness
From ourselves, for ourselves?[147]

An aspect of this attraction to a nonpaternal man is his capacity to function in a discriminating way. Because the Logos functions of separation and discrimination are often projected in the early stages of feminine development, the first partner chosen by the girl/woman is often someone unlike her own family—a stranger, rebel or someone with definite opinions and tastes who establishes her as different, introduces her to something new and sets her to thinking for herself.

A man who surpasses others in strength or power, whether physical, verbal, intellectual or spiritual, has a definite advantage in attracting women at this stage. His belief in his own uniqueness will draw her attention away from the paternal world.

Emma Jung posited four stages of animus development and their projected personifications in actual men. Including the father in her

---

[147] "As Difference Blends into Identity," in Ellman and O'Clair, *Norton Anthology,* p. 830.

first stage,[148] her classification might fit here. We might estimate the maturity of the woman's animus by her attraction to heroes of these types. Masculinity could be reflected in proving one's physical strength, then in initiating and asserting oneself (which predominates in this period), later in finding one's own words, or intellectual expression, and finally in spiritual strength.

A lively spirit is necessary to break the psychological bond with the father. This is not to imply that the girl/woman is a passive victim. These energies are in fact her own, and the man she encounters in the outer world and attaches herself to is the object of projection of these energies. Without the inner drive to individuate, she would remain tied to mother or father, no matter how many men she encountered. Louise Bogan's poem, "A Tale," inspired by her decision to marry and move to Panama, personifies her newly found independence and capacity for detachment as a "youth":

> This youth too long has heard the break
> Of waters in a land of change.
> He goes to see what suns can make
> From soil more indurate and strange.
>
> He cuts what holds his days together
> And shuts him in, as lock on lock:
> The arrowed vane announcing weather,
> The tripping racket of a clock;
>
> Seeking, I think, a light that waits
> Still as a lamp upon a shelf,—
> A land with hills like rocky gates
> Where no sea leaps upon itself.
>
> But he will find that nothing dares
> To be enduring, save where, south
> Of hidden deserts, torn fire glares
> On beauty with a rusted mouth,—
>
> Where something dreadful and another
> Look quietly upon each other.[149]

---

148 See above, p. 63.
149 See Elizabeth Frank, *Louise Bogan: A Portrait,* pp. 54-58.

The subject of many dreams and stories is the female task to find a suitor spirited enough to take her from the parental milieu. Being swept away by the fascinating otherness of the lover is a frequent experience in early unions and outweighs such factors as social background. The Romeo-and-Juliet theme is one image of this stage of development. For some women—and men—it is never outgrown. I remember a powerful dream of this period; in the dream I was literally carried away on the shoulders of my lover while an old man and a young girl were left behind, unable to catch up to us. The father and the Kore energies were surpassed by my hero, and obliterated my "better judgment" and innocence. Later my task would be to return for these abandoned aspects of myself.

Even after passing through the various stages, we retain their energies as part of our history and experience. Nothing in the psyche is thoroughly outgrown or killed off, but comes in and out of focus. Like early instinctual drives, these energies in some newly invigorating form can add spice to relationships. There are times in any healthy relationship when one or the other can enjoy parenting or being parented, romanticizing or primitivizing the interaction. It is characteristic at this stage that the relationship be romanticized, and the woman is unable to look directly and objectively at its real nature. As Adrienne Rich wrote, "A life I didn't choose chose me; even my tools are the wrong ones for what I have to do."[150]

Poetry expressing heroic and romantic partnership is heard continually in popular songs. Such powerful energy is involved in this stage of individuation that it is said to make the world go round. It is the precursor of the true coniunctio. Loss of romantic love is a prominent factor in adolescent suicides.

Anna Akhmatova captures the bewitching nuances of romance, the obsessive thoughts that distract us from everything else, the magic of nature's ordinary movements, the changes of mood, the anticipation:

Evening hours at the desk.
And a page irreparably white.
The mimosa calls up the heat of Nice,
a large bird flies in a beam of moonlight.

---

[150] "The Roofwalker," *Poems: Selected and New, 1950-1974*, pp. 63-64.

And having braided my hair carefully for the night
as if tomorrow braids will be necessary,
I look out the window, no longer sad,
at the sea, the sandy slopes.

What power a man has
who doesn't ask for tenderness!
I cannot lift my tired eyes
when he speaks my name.[151]

An aspect of this stage of partnership is its actual tenuousness in the face of its felt permanence. The ambivalence, the sense of risk-taking, the fear of the intrusion of the mundane into the realm of possibility and idealization, are described by Adrienne Rich:

She had thought the studio would keep itself;
no dust upon the furniture of love.
Half heresy, to wish the taps less vocal,
the panes relieved of grime. A plate of pears,
a piano with a Persian shawl, a cat
stalking the picturesque amusing mouse
had risen at his urging.
Not that at five each separate stair would writhe
under the milkman's tramp; that morning light
so coldly would delineate the scraps
of last night's cheese and three sepulchral bottles;
that on the kitchen shelf among the saucers
a pair of beetle-eyes would fix her own—
envoy from some black village in the mouldings . . .
Meanwhile, he, with a yawn,
sounded a dozen notes upon the keyboard,
declared it out of tune, shrugged at the mirror,
rubbed at his beard, went out for cigarettes;
while she, jeered by the minor demons,
pulled back the sheets and made the bed and found
a towel to dust the tabletop,
and let the coffee-pot boil over on the stove.
By evening she was back in love again,
though not so wholly but throughout the night

---

151 "Evening," *Twenty Poems,* p. 11.

she woke sometimes to feel the daylight coming
like a relentless milkman up the stairs.[152]

The excitement of sexual awakening belongs to this stage, perhaps
to last throughout the rest of life:

A flame from each finger,
my hands are candelabra,
my hair stands in a torch.
Out of my mouth a long flame hovers.
Can't anyone see, handing me a newspaper?
Can't anyone see, stamping my book overdue?
I walk blazing along Sixth Avenue,
burning gas blue I buy subway tokens,
a bouquet of coals, I cross the bridge.
Invisible I singe strangers and pass.
Now I am on your street.
How your window flickers.
I come bringing my burning body
like an armful of tigerlilies,
like a votive lantern,
like a roomful of tassels and leopards and grapes
for you to come into,
dance in my burning
and we will flare up together like stars
and fall to sleep.[153]

Relationships formed at this developmental level are always felt to
be eternal and yet are doomed to implosion. No relationship can en-
dure as long as one partner is carrying significant energies for the
other. Yet most marriages begin this way, with the potential to move
through romance to true intimacy with awareness. But awareness is
inhibited by various devices: denial, infidelity, alcohol abuse, etc.
Divorce is an easy escape from individuation when the pressure for
consciousness reaches uncomfortable proportions.

In "The Flute," Madeline Tiger describes what often occurs when
the adoring woman in a patriarchal partnership begins to need some-

---

[152] "Living in Sin," *Poems: Selected and New, 1950-1974*, pp. 18-19.
[153] Marge Piercy, "I Am a Light You Could Read By," *Circles on the Water*,
p. 50.

thing for herself. If a man expects to be mirrored continually by women, he may not be able to sustain any other kind of interaction:

> "I heard his breath in my sleep.
> My dream filled with his face."
> (and for Lucy)

> I heard his thinnest thought,
> believing us dear
> as tender animals
> the forest encloses
> and more than the fierce ones
> fierce; I held him
> and I heard his mother's death—
> how she gasped, she was
> so weak she couldn't
> call him from the back,
> his father had to
> announce the arrival of death
> in front, behind the register

> I heard the tombstone grow
> around his painting,
> his memory sealed
> inside a ribbed thing
> buried in back of little rooms
> on Archer Street

> But when my voice abruptly
> interrupted all that
> silent stuff, he left,
> so that I shouldn't hear
> this thing untwisting from
> its life-long death into
> wakeful sleep/half sleep;
> that I shouldn't crush the
> little flute no matter what
> no matter what I needed
> to be nourished by.[154]

---

[154] Unpublished.

It is at this point that a woman can thoroughly experience her need to establish and defend the yin-ego. She begins to realize that her values, mind and biological needs are not only likely to be quite different from her partner's but also equally valuable. She begins to claim not only *a* mind, but *her* mind, and to trust her instincts.

In spite of her belief that the new partnership in the outer world is eternal, new awareness will lead to loss of projections onto the partner. What is eternal is the inner experience, the awareness of the masculine principle in oneself. The archetype is eternal, not our identification with it inwardly or outwardly; it will remain, no matter what we go through. This is where happily ever after ends and a new story begins.

The new story begins in the woman with an equal partnership with her own inner man. No longer dependent on outer men for her existence, she looks within for sustenance. The effect of this in the outer world is to create a greater interest in the partner's personal qualities, rather than his ability to rescue her or do things for her. The effect in the inner world is to experience calm and courage.

11
Equal Partner

We must sit down
and reason together.
We must sit down.
Men standing want to hold forth.
They rain down upon faces lifted.

. . . .

The men must bother to listen.

The women must learn to say, I think this is so.

The men must learn to stop dancing solos on the ceiling.
After each speaks, she or he
will repeat a ritual phrase:

It is not I who speaks but the wind.
Wind blows through me.
Long after me, is the wind.

—Marge Piercy, from "Councils."

After late adolescence, the possibility that was foreseen in the stage
of the hero/heroine can be actualized; that is, the male principle,
heretofore explored and experienced primarily in outer relationships,
can be contemplated by the woman as her inner partner.

How simple to say! How difficult to live! In the words of Marie-
Louise von Franz, "To integrate the anima or animus is a master-
piece, and nobody can claim to have succeeded."[155] Personally I
prefer the term "relate to" rather than "integrate." We are free to relate
to and participate in the energy of the archetypes. By no means does

---

[155] *Shadow and Evil in Fairytales,* p. 5. Jung made a similar observation:
"If the encounter with the shadow is the 'apprentice-piece' in the individual's development, then that with the anima is the 'master-piece.'" ("Archetypes of the Collective Unconscious," *The Archetypes and the Collective
Unconscious,* CW 9i, par. 61)

the ego ever integrate the animus. He is always more or less auton-omous; now, in the stage of equal partner, his presence as an intra-psychic figure predominates.

Within the past few hours two women have spoken about their lives in terms of lessons to be learned. It is not uncommon for sev-eral patients to pick up on one theme in one day. Is it in me? Is it in the air? Just coincidence?

The first said, "I thought with age the lessons would get easier be-cause I would be smarter. But no! the lessons are getting harder!" When the second said, "My life seems to be a series of lessons to be learned," I asked, "Do you believe the lessons are getting harder?" She thought long. "Not harder, but subtler." "Really?" This woman has come through a divorce, a life-threatening case of asthma and surgery for cancer within three years. "Even though I seem to be getting hit hard, over and over, it feels like something is trying to get my attention; actually the lessons are peeling off gradually, like the fine skin of an onion. Some things are harder, but my ties to impor-tant people are getting stronger."

The experience of continually unfolding is the curse and privilege of those who choose to individuate. Gradually, more of the inner world is exposed and the interplay between the inner masculine and feminine becomes apparent.

As with other stages, this one is approached with feelings of both excitement and regret. What could ever move us out of the stage of wine and roses that the patriarchal partner offers? The promise of autonomy? The thrill of creative drives finally coming to fruition? The hope of building a better world? Perhaps. Some do sail smooth-ly into this world on the winds of fame or grace or an indomitable creative spirit.

More often I see women turning to confrontation for their survival only after some life crisis: moral conflict, a failed relationship, an empty nest, illness, accident, a death in the family, old age, aban-donment, financial or professional failure. Then we are driven to look within for a new attitude to life or new way of relating. Then we begin preparing seriously for the inner marriage.

Moving into the stage of equal partner is a crucial transition, years in the making, not limited to heterosexuals or women. Struggles with romanticism and sexuality take many forms: the successful who have everything and know it is not enough; the man who craves intimacy from a hostile wife; the loving wife with her alcoholic husband; the beautiful lesbian with her aging partner; the faithful priest with his blatantly seductive admirers; the doctors whom patients exploit; the patients whom doctors exploit; the love-starved young sated with banal sex; spirited women with sick or impotent partners; the loyal who love the faithless; the faithless who crave the unattainable.

By whatever route we come to it, whatever it may look like, this stage involves seeing though our penchant for concretizing the drive for union. Taking back the projections that were put onto the other, we accept the fact that we have all we need in ourselves. Maybe not all we want, but all we need. A crucial question for many women is whether an intimate relationship with animus precludes loving an outer partner. It certainly does not, but rather enhances all connections eventually.[156]

The exciting part is that in intimate partnership we can love each other better than ever! However, there are some dangers to relatedness in the early phases of becoming self-empowered. It is possible to assume the qualities associated with the patriarchal man, applying a kind of drive toward relationship that is more ambitious than related, a blinding light of openness which leads to unrealistic expectations of others. Marriages and relationships may shrivel in this light. A woman who became a lawyer for reasons which appealed to her animus, said she had to look in the mirror every day and steel herself for another day in court; her strong feminine identity rejected the role. Unbalanced animus energy may tend to objectify and depersonalize, leading to materialistic or coldly selfish attitudes. Or, even if the woman is well balanced in expressing herself, the outer partner may envy and resent the increased consciousness that relating to the animus confers on a woman, and seek out a less aware partner who presents no challenge. Partners who can accept the challenge of awareness and unfold together reap rich rewards.

Giving value to relatedness is basic to the feminine soul. In a patriarchal society the fundamental desire to love and be loved is ex-

---

156 See James Hillman, *Anima,* pp. 115-127, on literalism in the heroic attitude toward integrating anima and animus.

pressed consciously through the feminine and unconsciously through the masculine. Men claim to be independent, but act out dependency on women. Women openly express dependency but function as containing mothers or indispensable possessions to men. The desire for true relatedness is mistaken for dependency and is demeaned, and those who openly express such desires may be labeled "insecure" or "needy," having the unfulfilled needs of the less-conscious projected upon them.

This dynamic can be seen in the confusion that plagues the mental health professions around the concepts of co-dependence and masochism. The confusion results from simplistically reducing affiliative needs to an absence of inner resources, instead of appreciating the positive valence of desire, emanating from psychological richness. Authentic loving signifies abundance, not deprivation.

While the unconscious animus interferes with relatedness, the animus when confronted can be an asset. Some introversion is implied in the withdrawal of projections from men and coming to an experience of equal partnership. In stories depicting female individuation there is always a period of ego-surrender and introversion during which the woman learns to care for and love herself by discovering the deepest core of her feminine being. The years alone in the forest or desert, or exiled among strangers, symbolize the retreat into oneself to make this psychological and spiritual transition.

Crucial in the relationship with animus now is the capacity to allow him to be a helpmate in the further descent to the center of the feminine experience, and also the return to the world with the treasured feminine. As we saw previously, Emily Dickinson was able to call upon the positive animus and turn with renewed ferocity to poetry writing when faced with a major rejection. Instead of depression, she experienced a creative and lasting liberation.

This is our task as women today; to recognize and articulate the place of the animus in this stage of development. If anima mediates the possibility of reflection,[157] animus mediates the possibility of articulation of the unconscious. I see the animus as a helpmate in the process of individuation, whatever the path, lending to the inner

---

[157] Ibid., p. 85.

work discipline, energy to act with initiative, objectivity, spirit, courage to face the unknown, and determination. As mediator of the unknown he represents a commitment to consciousness, helping us to value, to differentiate, to stand aside and question that which eludes consciousness. Stimulating through the excitement of otherness, he fertilizes the imagination, respects mystery, assists in understanding messages from the Self.

The animus's form of guidance varies with the typology of the individual. I, a feeling type, perceive that he helps me to be attentive in mental work, and also that he is very involved with the kingdoms of Time and Order. What holds up as consistently masculine inside myself is an orientation to the future; early on I was aware of living in a timeless present, which was later challenged by the dawning of animus energy. Oriented toward future, he glories in preparedness. I experience a certain determination in remembering, and particularly recording dreams, that feels masculine. I believe he helps me to be firm in taking care of my body, to guard my time and energy, to say "no" to flighty distractions and petty intrigue, to delay gratification, to pay attention to my own ideas and intuitions, to commit myself to my decisions, to be clear in dialogues with myself and others.

On the dark side, he has his own petty ambitions and pedantry, is unreasonable on questions of chronos-time, and is usually around with his orderliness when I am being compulsive and uncompromising. He also lends energy to sarcasm and cynicism, which I will explain later in an example of active imagination with "King Friday."

Women in this stage experience advantages that compensate for the loss of innocence and idealization of the previous stages. The mature inner partner lends a sense of responsibility as a privilege, rather than a burden. Questions of integrity, while not necessarily easy, are challenges, not nightmares. I don't mean to paint a picture that life is all bliss, but we no longer have to suffer from the curse of being imperfect; a few faults are allowed us. We don't panic at the thought of eating and sleeping alone. We look forward to whatever it is we are involved in, and with more pleasure and less ambivalence than before. We feel autonomous, no one's puppet, experience the fruits of our creativity, find the energy to try to build a better world, cling to life as a root, even to the barest soil. We realize that we never have to live with deception, or humiliation, or overbearing, self-serving partners, unless we really want to. We can choose passion or security and sometimes both or neither.

Some in this stage of life choose to stay with partners they have resented for years. The question of the partner's adequacy—as provider, lover, parent, manager, whatever—looms less large; other factors take priority when the inner partner is in place. Some are able to actualize a grand duet with an equal partner in outer life. Some choose to invest their energy in a personal project rather than squander it on partners who cannot meet them as equals. Some believe that celibacy is a necessary state for completing the final spiritual passage. Living out of the animus relationship can take many forms, reflecting the many emanations of the universal masculine.

What is the equal partner in the outer world like? A good bit of my time is spent listening to what women admire in men. A composite might include the capacity for intimate talking and listening, but also self-sufficiency and the ability to tolerate aloneness without undue anxiety.

The equal male partner can allow us our own space (career, children, art, etc.) without needing to escape from himself through another companion or some form of addictive behavior. He has his own creative work. He does not need us to mother him, keep him straight or provide a nest from which to roam, as does the mother-bound man. He does not need us to be his perfect ornament or mirror or worshipful appendage, as does the father-bound man. He does not need us to compete with each other in beauty, sexuality and accomplishments, as does the patriarchal partner.

The equal partner can enjoy our emotionality and sexuality without shriveling, folding, dissolving or running in terror to a less differentiated position or partner. He sees us and likes us and can put up with what he doesn't like. He is not so frightened of getting old that he looks only at younger faces and bodies. He understands that sickness and death accompany life, and does not run from them. He understands that children are younger and more vulnerable than adults and need lots of patience. He can distinguish patience from passivity and cowardice. He understands that we are not the cause of, or responsible for, his moods. He understands that true intimacy means negotiating, not just ventilating, negative feelings and thoughts. He is not scared of the dark. He wants to be known. He can love, work, stay, play and see. His energy may reflect any one of Robert Moore's masculine archetypes—lover, warrior, king or magus—or Edward Whitmont's or Jean Bolen's "gods"[158]—but the desired qualities can be represented in all developed types.

At this stage active imagination becomes particularly meaningful. Poetry as an introspective tool is not just reactive but a process of concentration and internal dialogue supported by animus energy. Poetry can amplify any dream image or psychic content. Here I have chosen to show how poetry can amplify animus images.

One woman, for example, finding herself in a bad mood for no apparent reason on a quiet Sunday morning, decided to observe the inner voices and record them. There were mainly two: a pleasant, feminine voice that gladly cooperated with the usual rituals—her familiar self—and a bad-natured, complaining, critical voice, which she personified as a "red-neck":

> The way he leaves the bed
> (nothing's been said)
> shows he's already mean.
> He doesn't want food;
> . . . .
> he needs to break something
> to match something broken inside.
> Somewhere deep
> in the back of his skull
> a glimpse of kindness
> flits across his memory
> like a frightened moth,
> still trapped in the past
> and seldom seen.

As the poem emerged, this woman began to see the repressed pain and fear behind her bad mood. Since they were not consciously experienced by her female ego, she surmised that they might be due to frustrated attempts to express her masculine energies. Looking

---

158 See Whitmont, *Return of the Goddess;* Moore, *King, Warrior, Magician, Lover*; Bolen, *Gods in Everyman.*

deeper, she saw that she harbored a male counterpart who was afraid to believe in kindness. This was the beginning of a process of understanding her puzzling mood swings. One might argue that the same process could occur without personifying the mood as masculine; nevertheless, the image presented itself in male form, which greatly facilitated catching the mood and speaking to it.

Jayne Bucy, in the process of objectifying a relationship, wrote the following poem which helped her to discern aspects of the relationship that were her responsibility. The inner partner who collaborated with her in the writing helped her to see the knife-wielder and the gypsy in herself, as well as the poet-ego.

> I would snatch the knife
> from your hand
> before it slices through
> our string of days
> my heart like a rabbit
> in my chest
>
> Instead, I float up
> through the roof
> of my mouth
> into the sky
> where the air is too blue
> to breathe
>
> Your ice eyes turn
> into her many colors
> and all you want is the gypsy
> as she weaves herself
> around your waist[159]

Sometimes it is possible to trace the exact incident which caused the pain, through images that come alive in a poem. For example, a woman had a series of dreams and poems with a "desperado" theme. Desperado became more and more palpable; she began to anticipate when he would show up in her moods and interactions. At times he was mean and sadistic, at times clever and humorous, and at yet other times rash and hurried.

---

[159] "Gypsy Desire" (unpublished).

After a while she learned that her reaction to the slightest degree of rejection, even the expectation of it, was to slip into a subtle but predictable manic state. This was applauded by the world, who saw it as good humor; rarely did anyone suspect it was a defense against anticipated pain. Who would imagine that a chronically cheerful attitude harbored a desperate phantom? Through the attention to Desperado, she learned to avoid defensive maneuvers and respond more authentically to perceived woundings. Once the manic reaction was identified as a response to a specific stimulus, it lost its potency. For a while, depressive feelings became more noticeable; also, ordinary feelings of well-being were not recognized as pleasant because they didn't carry the anxious excitement of Desperado.

Gradually, Desperado disappeared from this woman's dreams and ego-states. By then she was very sensitized to seeing his energy working in other people. She also remembered a significant man in her life who had swept her up in his manic moods. She realized she was drawn to any man with this characteristic, regardless of other factors in his personality. By exploring the feelings of sadism and recklessness when they came up in her, she was able to contain them rather than act them out compulsively. Through this process, her ego gained access to the energy that was projected onto this animus figure and could put it to creative use.

Another woman had trouble controlling her tendency to blow up in situations which seemed fairly innocuous. One night she dreamed of a man throwing firecrackers. She wrote:

> . . . you scatter fire, sober as a farmer
> sowing his field, or feeding his fowl.
> With your close-clipped hair
> and Germanic ways you go, incongruous,
> tossing your gifts of energy around us.
> The mother in me wants to kill you,
> but the child follows you with glee,
> and you notice neither of us
> as you go on, casting for terror.

This is a good example of how a poem can write itself and give new information. Until she wrote the poem the dreamer did not know that 1) the man was Germanic, 2) he reminded her of her farming ancestors, 3) she was wrathful toward him, 4) her inner child delighted in him. She *had* recognized that his lack of feeling and his playing with fire had something to do with terrorism. This one dream and poem gave us enough analytic material to work on for weeks, and resulted in a breakthrough in her understanding of her temper tantrums and their relationship to her creative animus.

A woman who was working on tolerating her lover's adolescent son wrote poems to the boy, which she never shared with him. She only exposed them in analysis. The poem-boy took on a surrealistic quality and over a period of months was transformed into an adult and loving animus figure. Concurrently, the relationship with her lover and his son improved.

In my own case, I worked for some time on an extremely narcissistic complex, which I named "King Friday" after the puppet-king on the children's television program "Mr. Rogers' Neighborhood." I was always tickled by the king's exhorting his subjects in such a patient, long-suffering tone of voice: "Be perfect; that's all I ask!" It touched an old familiar patriarchal chord. A poem helped me get in touch with the dynamics of this complex, and revealed that I protected my narcissism by refusing to ask questions at times when curiosity was called for. I was depriving myself of information essential to my well-being, and out of a stubborn and fearful pride of which I had been completely unconscious. All this information, plus the concern with time, came with the poem. Here are a few lines:

> It is hard in the dark, even for princes,
> unless you look long and hard and know
> through owl eyes.
> A wounded child, afraid of memory, cannot ask, "Why?"
> If you challenge him he walks away wordless.
> A wounded child, remembering, is like an owl;
> he is still and through slow blinks
> he sees into the dark.
>
> (later, in early adulthood)
> He flew through life like a bullet
> leaving large holes to be filled by others.
> His queen was always crying, "Wait!"
> But he sped through,

so as not to come late
to being perfect.
His children ran to keep up;
they felt they must,
as only the weight of lust
could slow him.

The wounded child, remembering, can ask for information and apply strategy to an emotional issue.

One way in which the animus mediates the unconscious is by inciting us to question it, to differentiate its contents, not to "swallow the poem whole." This is often a matter of typology: the animus brings up the other side. Personally, as a feeling type, the animus has helped me to learn to ask questions, argue and formulate opinions, when my natural bent is to see all sides inconclusively. Thinking types, on the other hand, may need the animus to consider the feeling consequences of following an argument to its logical conclusion; he may give a woman the strength to contain, not express, the need to persist "at all cost."[160] The animus can bring an intuitive woman down to earth and enable a sensation type to fly.[161]

The following poems illustrate the fruits of inner work in the development of an animus partner who is an authentic equal—not an idealization or an object to be feared, but a person who can be spoken to honestly with one's whole voice. The voice may transmit joy, love, fear, anger—any human emotion. The crux of the matter is that anything human can be tolerated in this relationship; any interaction is grist for the mill of continuing dialogue and growing awareness. By contemplating these masculine features, the poets enrich the contact between the inner feminine and masculine. Poet Jean Burden wrote that the artist is psychologically androgynous, creating from the polarity inherent in one's masculine and feminine natures. She sees the creative act in women as essentially expressive of a mascu-

---

[160] The question of how animus, traditionally the principle of Logos, functions in a thinking-type woman is a major theme of *The Woman in the Mirror* by Claire Douglas, who points out the unreasonableness of identifying the thinking and feeling processes with a particular gender.
[161] See Daryl Sharp, *Personality Types: Jung's Model of Typology,* for an overview of the different types.

line drive. "Whenever I write a poem I have to gather myself into the masculine side of me and thrust into the feminine side. The result is a poem."[162]

Claudia Lapp, describing the process of translating dreams into poetry, wrote, "From the first words we are editing, interpreting, making—like it or not—symbol out of image." The recording of dreams and the writing of poems require different functions. The translation becomes easier, she says, when we have "faith in the validity of perceptions from the unconscious." (I see this as a function of the positive animus.) She recommends learning to shift the focus of consciousness through meditation and practices such as nondominant-hand writing.[163]

This poem by Lapp celebrates the chthonic, natural man, unadorned by the trappings of civilization and very much a consort, not a pawn, of the Earth Mother. She wrote it with Robert Bly especially in mind.[164]

> i love a man
> with some wildness left in him,
> a space evergreen dark
> where nothing's programmed,
> where hair's unkempt and
> bodies know bodies by
> skin scents and fur signals
>
> i don't mean sex only—
> i mean the space evergreen dark
> where anything might happen,
> the moist grasses

---

[162] In Jean Gould, *Modern American Women Poets,* p. 260n.

[163] Personal communication, 1980.

[164] Many women, including myself, are grateful to Bly for his efforts to help men recover qualities they have repressed. In an interview for Sounds True of Boulder, Bly said, "At the base of the masculine psyche there is a very clear and luminous structure which looks as if it's made up of an interlocking of the King, the Warrior, the Lover, the Wildman, the Trickster, maybe the Quester or Magician. . . . If you're interested in wildness, then the task would be to get down to that level where the wildman is, or where the wild woman is. . . . The effort should be to do that descent oneself. . . . The wildman is going to be on the other side of grief, not on this side of it." ("The Descent into Ourselves," p. 24)

> where he is pleased to walk alone
> with the darkness and his own weight,
> where he's conversing with bark or stone,
> rooted at the mound of the earth [165]

Here is a masculine image quite different from the typical yang-male of sun-sky. The symbol itself is valuable as it expands the possibilities of grounding the masculine. Often the animus is pictured as soaring, carrying one to great heights, but as mediator of the unconscious he can also accompany us into the instinctual realm. In the above poem, I like Lapp's ability to hold the image and develop it; she relishes physicality and sensuousness, differentiated beyond mere sexuality. She appreciates the man's solitary nature. She has to have been there, close to and loving her own instinctual life and willing to accept it as something beyond her ego, an eternal quality to be shared with a man.

Equal partnership allows for broad expressiveness, not merely polite, persona-based adaptation. The developed woman wants to give and receive love, which does not mean she is helpless. She wants to express disagreement and disapproval, which is not to say she seeks to dominate and control. She wants to express compassion and vulnerability, which doesn't obviate enjoying competition and aggression, qualities of the grounded masculine.

Denise Levertov captures several aspects of the inner masculine: the historical animus, both from her personal history and from cultures past; the collaborative animus who supports the poet's creative process; and the spiritual agent who knows the mystery in "the pause of a needle."

> The Rav
> of Northern White Russia declined,
> in his youth, to learn the
> language of the birds, because
> the extraneous did not interest him; nevertheless
> when he grew old it was found
> he understood them anyway, having
> listened well, and as it is said, 'prayed

---

[165] "Wildermann," *Cloud Gate,* p. 2.

with the bench and the floor.' He used
what was at hand—as did
Angel Jones of Mold, whose meditations
were sewn into coats and britches.
    Well , I would like to make,
thinking some line still taut between me and them,
poems direct as what the birds said,
hard as a floor, sound as a bench,
mysterious as the silence when the tailor
would pause with his needle in the air.[166]

In "Tecumseh," Mary Oliver demonstrates how we choose our spiritual family and take up their values. Though one may not have actual Indian ancestors, the animus in the form of an Indian guide can be a strong force in renewing a woman's reverence for the Earth.

I went down not long ago
to the Mad River, under the willows
I knelt and drank from that crumpled flow, call it
what madness you will, there's a sickness
worse than the risk of death and that's
forgetting what we should never forget.
Tecumseh lived here.
The wounds of the past
are ignored, but hang on
like the litter that snags among the yellow branches,
newspapers and plastic bags, after the rains.

Where are the Shawnee now?
Do you know? Or would you have to
write to Washington, and even then,
whatever they said,
would you believe it? Sometimes

---

[166] "Illustrious Ancestors," in Ellman and O'Clair, *Norton Anthology,* pp. 1060-1061. A biography of Levertov states that she "has been proud to claim a connection with mystics of the past. Her father was descended from a Russian rabbi . . . renowned as a Hasid, that is, as a member of a Jewish mystical movement that began in the 18th century and found a glory in everyday occurrences rather than in sensational events. He was reputed, as she tells in *Overland to the Islands,* to know the speech of birds. Her mother was descended from the Welsh tailor and mystic, Angel Jones of Mold." (Ibid., p. 1056)

I would like to paint my body red and go out into
the glittering snow
to die.

His name meant Shooting Star.
From Mad River country north to the border
he gathered the tribes
and armed them one more time. He vowed
to keep Ohio and it took him
over twenty years to fail.

After the bloody and final fighting, at Thames
it was over, except
his body could not be found.
It was never found,
and you can do whatever you want with that, say

his people came in the black leaves of the night
and hauled him to a secret grave, or that
he turned into a little boy again, and leaped
into a birch canoe and went
rowing home down the rivers. Anyway,
this much I'm sure of: if we ever meet him, we'll know it,
he will still be
so angry.[167]

There are many poems in which women describe their connection
with a famous figure or personal mentor. We can see them as ways
of recognizing and communicating with the partner within, in his
specific areas of talent. It can be argued that some of these poems are
influenced by the hero animus, but the process of identifying and differentiating these "talents" is done with the cooperation of a more
evolved inner partner. For example, Gwendolyn Brooks wrote:

There is a little lightning in his eyes.
Iron at the mouth.
His brows ride neither too far up nor down.
He is splendid. With a place to stand.

Some glowing in the common blood.

---

[167] *American Primitive,* p. 77.

Some specialness within.[168]

Oliver appreciates the patient work of her mentor, Stanley Kunitz:

> I used to imagine him
> coming from the house, like Merlin
> strolling with important gestures
> through the garden
>
> . . . .
>
> But now I know more
> about the great wheel of growth,
> and decay, and rebirth,
> and know my vision for a falsehood.
> Now I see him coming from the house—
> I see him on his knees,
> cutting away the diseased, the superfluous,
> coaxing the new,
> knowing that the hour of fulfillment
> is buried in years of patience—
> yet willing to labor like that
> on the mortal wheel.
>
> Oh, what good it does the heart
> to know it isn't magic![169]

Inspired by his book, *A Brief History of Time,* I wrote "A Dance with Hawking":

> How I love dancing
> in the bright music of your light . . .
> When you lift me
> on your mind's manly arm
> we glide over galaxies
> into the forgotten future
> of this cosmic comedy
> where all our small failings are fertile.
> Hawking, you gleam of Shiva,
> wind your scintillating scarf

168 Gwendolyn Brooks, "Of Robert Frost," in Ellman and O'Clair, *Norton Anthology,* p. 950.
169 Mary Oliver, from "Stanley Kunitz," *Dream Work,* p. 44.

of energy around me
and I will leap into
a million million million waves of your
pulsating spirit.

Sages are typical animus figures of the equal partner stage, and poems to or about them are common. Here are two by Denise Levertov:

With certitude
Simeon opened
ancient arms
to infant light.
Decades
before the cross, the tomb
and the new life,
he knew
new life.
What depth
of faith he drew on,
turning illumined
towards deep night.[170]

Trust is the key in Simeon, as in this man:

A man growing old is going
down the dark stairs.
He has been speaking of the Soul
tatooed with the Law.
Of dreams
burnt in the bone.

He looks up
to the friends who lean
out of light and wine
over the well of stairs.
They ask his pardon
for the dark they can't help.
Starladen Babylon
buzzes in his blood, an ancient

---

[170] "Candlemas," *Breathing the Water,* p. 70.

pulse. The rivers
run out of Eden.
Before Adam
Adam blazes.

'It's alright,' answers
the man going down.
'It's alright—there are many
avenues, many corridors of the soul
that are dark also.
Shalom.'[171]

Marriage, the most potent symbol of the coniunctio, is exalted
when the spouses attain true intimacy. It is always satisfying to find
a marriage that reflects true partnership.

The ache of marriage:

thigh and tongue, beloved,
are heavy with it,
it throbs in the teeth

We look for communion
and are turned away, beloved,
each and each

It is leviathan and we
in its belly
looking for joy, some joy
not to be known outside it

two by two in the ark of
the ache of it.[172]

What is clear here is that a tension between the need for union and
the need for individuality permeates marriage, creating joy and pain.
An authentic feminine attribute, I believe, is the capacity to hold joy
and pain as essential parts of any experience.

Inside of me
is a poppy, wide open petals

---

[171] "Shalom," in Ellman and O'Clair, *Norton Anthology,* pp. 1064-1065.

[172] Denise Levertov, "The Ache of Marriage," ibid., p. 1064.

weighted in gold,
waiting for your breath
to scatter me on the wind.

Inside of me
is a doe, velvet soft,
brown eyes watchful,
waiting to bound, free,
over rotting logs of past
to put one cloven hoof
on your green meadowgrass
and feed on you.

Inside of me
is a smoldering ember,
banked, waiting, sheltered,
ready to explode in brilliant light
and heat and crackling flame,
should you fan, carefully,
knowingly, should you care
to share the warmth
of ecstasy with me.[173]

Of course, marriage has many moods, like the sea, and here Anne Spencer speaks to the mate from whom death cannot separate her:

Maker-of-Sevens in the scheme of things
From earth to star;
Thy cycle holds whatever is fate, and
Over the border the bar.
Though rank and fierce the mariner
Sailing the seven seas,
He prays, as he holds his glass to his eyes,
Coaxing the Pleiades.
. . . .
But I can wait the seven of moons,
Or years I spare,
Hoarding the heart's plenty, nor spend
A drop, nor share—
So long but outlives a smile and

---

[173] Glenda Taylor, "For My Husband," *Life Is a River,* p. 29.

A silken gown;
Then gaily I reach up from my shroud,
And you, glory-clad, reach down.[174]

In the following poem, Teresa of Avila speaks of the spiritual
marriage. In distinguishing between imaginative and intellectual vision, she acknowledges that the fantasy of coniunctio and the experience of it occur on different levels. The true coniunctio, or inner marriage, takes place beyond ego-consciousness, imparting immersion
in a life of grace which has no need for fantasies of union.

> ... this secret union takes place
> in the very interior of the soul
> which must be where God is.
> There is no need of any door for God to enter.
> . . . .
> That which comes to pass
> in the union of the spiritual marriage
> is very different.
> The Lord appears in the center of the soul,
> not in an imaginative vision
> but in an intellectual one,
> although more delicate than those mentioned,
> as he appeared to the apostles
> without entering through the door
> when he said to them
> "Peace be with you."[175]

Transiting the stage of the equal partner (Neumann's "True Confrontation") to the feminine Self and androgynous animus is an experience I cannot presume to describe fully. As we move toward actual-
izing wisdom we may grasp intuitively its qualities, found in the
beauty and dignity of wise women and men. We move in and out of
this wisdom during a lifetime, catching brief glimpses of it. Haven't
we all been humbled by the Self revealed in the precocious insights
of a child? Artists, poets and mystics carry us to the lap of the
Goddess to preview our possibilities.

---

[174] "The Wife-Woman," in Ellman and O'Clair, *Norton Anthology*, pp.
277-278.
[175] *Meditations with Teresa of Avila*, p. 116.

Annis McCabe, an intuitive artist, had a story present itself to her; she could barely write it down fast enough on scraps of paper and part of a window shade, as it came without warning.[176] I would say it was the animus who enabled her to grasp the opportunity, while the story itself came from the feminine Self.

Her story is essentially about the transformation of a mermaid to a bird, then to a human—an intuitive vision of woman's individuation process through the maternal sea and paternal sky to her complete nature incorporating all. It includes rich images of the union of opposites and several animus figures who bridge the worlds spanned by the transformation. It inspired a series of art works, including a sculpture of a crucified mermaid. Both the mermaid and the crucified woman appear often in women's imagery these days, a response to the growing awareness of the resurrection of the feminine in the collective consciousness.[177]

Ultimately, the exploration of animus leads us to the realization of the feminine side of the Self. To the extent to which we can anthropomorphize, some consistent qualities pervade the many attempts to define her. For example, she contains and unifies ever-changing qualities, is mutable as the moon or water, rather than consistent or linear. Hence, she manifests gradually in an atmosphere of stillness rather than action. Her realm is the present. She is revealed through processes of initiation that are personal experiences rather than courses of disciplined study. Coming to her requires descent, sacrifice of power, and the development of a personal morality and individuated spirituality.

Paradoxically, the feminine Self represents the humble and inferior in her fulsome glory while at the same time she renders the mundane sacred. Although she holds dear the value of relatedness, the way to her invariably involves loneliness, relinquishing of societal ties and coming, through faith in the inner man, to the center, as Hestia to the hearth. She takes us beyond the power of phallus and into the profundity of wombfullness.[178]

---

[176] "A Creation Story" (unpublished).

[177] See Julia Jewett, "Womansoul: A Feminine Corrective to Christian Imagery," and Nor Hall, *The Moon and the Virgin*, pp. 154-165.

[178] These qualities are gleaned from the writing of many women, including

Coming to the Goddess is not a once-in-a-lifetime descent, as some myths might lead us to believe. In my experience it is a continuing circle of descents and returns, gradually coming to know Her through Him, and vice versa.[179]

A quality of the androgyne stage of feminine development is the capacity to feel at one with humankind, without concerns about categories and hierarchies.

> Perhaps
> it's true, as you say,
> that after all these years,
> I don't know the first thing about you
> and you don't know me,
> and never will.
>
> Consciously.
>
> Perhaps
> it's true that, being me,
> I cannot plumb the depths of your being
> rich, black, Chicano, Sioux or Hebrew,
>
> Consciously.
>
> Perhaps
> it's true that whatever I say about me
> has nothing to do with you.
>
> Consciously.
>
> But, oh, beneath that
> iceberg of consciousness,
> the cerebral cortex of individual egohood,
>
> Life is a river,
> A vast current of pure energy,
> a cosmic floodtide of unity,
> a balanced and counterbalanced flow of Tao,

Claire Douglas, Joan Engleman, M. Esther Harding, Linda Leonard, Sylvia Brinton Perera and Marion Woodman.

[179] See Young-Eisendrath and Wiedemann, *Female Authority,* p. 145, on the developmental difference in the descent and return of Persephone, Psyche and Ariadne, and Sylvia Brinton Perera, *Descent to the Goddess.*

a hologram,
a universal, archetypal play of seeming opposites,
orchestrated by the Cosmic Self
to an all-containing, undivided, seamless,
omnipotent, whole and holy,
all-embracing, all known and knowing
One.

Perhaps
we will soon begin to know this

Consciously.[180]

The following two poems display the breadth of Denise Levertov's cosmic connection, first with an immigrant taxi driver—

Riding by taxi, Brooklyn to Queens,
a grey spring day. The Hispanic driver,
when I ask, 'Es usted Mexicano?' tells me
No, he's an exile from Uruguay. And I say,
'The only other Uruguayan I've met
was a writer—maybe
you know his name?—
            Mario Benedetti?'
  And he takes both hands
off the wheel and swings round,
glittering with joy. 'Benedetti!
Mario Benedetti!'
            There are
hallelujas in his voice—
we execute a perfect
figure 8 on the shining highway,
and rise aloft, high above traffic, flying
all the rest of the way in the blue sky, azul, azul![181]

—and here with unseen masculine forces:

A wanderer comes at last
to the forest hut where it was promised
someone wise would receive him.
And there's no one there; birds and small animals

---

180   Glenda Taylor, "Consciously," *Life Is a River,* p. 29.
181   "Poet Power," *Breathing the Water,* p. 56.

flutter and vanish, then return to observe.
No human eyes meet his.
But in the hut there's food,
set to keep warm beside glowing logs,
and fragrant garments to fit him, replacing
the rags of his journey,
and a bed of heather from the hills.
He stays there waiting. Each day the fire
is replenished, the pot refilled while he sleeps.
He draws up water from the well,
writes of his travels, listens for footsteps.
Little by little he finds
the absent sage is speaking to him,
is present.

       This is the way
you have spoken to me, the way—startled—
I find I have heard you. When I need it,
a book or a slip of paper
appears in my hand, inscribed by yours; messages
waiting on cellar shelves, in forgotten boxes
until I would listen.
       Your spirits relax;
now she is looking, you say to each other,
now she begins to see. [182]

The sacredness of all things finite, reflected upon by Marianne Moore, suggests the androgynous stage:

    What is our innocence,
what is our guilt? All are
    naked, none is safe. And whence
is courage: the unanswered question,
the resolute doubt —
    dumbly calling, deafly listening— that
is misfortune, even death,
        encourages others
        and in its defeat, stirs

    the soul to be strong? He

---

[182] "The Spirits Appeased," ibid, p. 8.

sees deep and is glad, who
    accedes to mortality
and in his imprisonment rises
upon himself as
the sea in a chasm, struggling to be
free and unable to be,
    in its surrendering
    finds its continuing.

So he who strongly feels,
behaves. The very bird,
    grown taller as he sings, steels
his form straight up. Though he is captive,
his mighty singing
says, satisfaction is a lowly
thing, how pure a thing is joy.
        This is mortality,
        this is eternity.[183]

The movement of animus energy is to the androgyne, the One, the "marvelous truth," as Levertov calls it in the following poem, "Matins." It is the truth that enables us to see the spirit in all things material, and the body enclosing each idea—the One in the other, the holy in the ordinary.

i

The authentic! Shadows of it
sweep past in dreams, one could say imprecisely,
evoking the almost-silent
ripping apart of giant
sheets of cellophane. No.
It thrusts up close. Exactly in dreams
it has you off-guard, you
recognize it before you have time.
For a second before waking
the alarm bell is a red conical hat, it
takes form.

---

[183] Marianne Moore, "What Are Years?" in Ellman and O'Clair, *Norton Anthology,* p. 428.

ii

The authentic! I said
rising from the toilet seat.
The radiator in rhythmic knockings
spoke of the rising steam.
The authentic, I said
breaking the handle of my hairbrush as I
brushed my hair in
rhythmic strokes: That's it,
that's joy, it's always
a recognition, the known
appearing fully itself, and
more itself than one knew.

iii

The new day rises
as heat rises,
knocking in the pipes
with rhythms it seizes for its own
to speak of its invention—
the real, the new-laid
egg whose speckled shell
the poet fondles and must break
if he will be nourished.

iv

A shadow painted where
yes, a shadow must fall.
The cow's breath
not forgotten in the mist, in the
words. Yes,
verisimilitude draws up
heat in us, zest
to follow through,
follow through,
follow
transformations of day
in its turning, in its becoming.

v

Stir the holy grains, set
the bowls on the table and
call the child to eat.

While we eat we think,
as we think an undercurrent
of dreams runs through us
faster than thought
towards recognition.

Call the child to eat,
send him off, his mouth
tasting of toothpaste, to go down
into the ground, into a roaring train
and to school.

His cheeks are pink
his black eyes hold his dreams, he has left
forgetting his glasses.

Follow down the stairs at a clatter
to give them to him and save
his clear sight.

Cold air
comes in at the street door.

vi

The authentic! It rolls
just out of reach, beyond
running feet and
stretching fingers, down
the green slope and into
the black waves of the sea.
Speak to me, little horse, beloved,
tell me
how to follow the iron ball,
how to follow through to the country
beneath the waves
to the place where I must kill you and you step out
of your bones and flystrewn meat

tall, smiling, renewed,
formed in your own likeness.

vii

Marvelous Truth, confront us
at every turn,
in every guise, iron ball,
egg, dark horse, shadow,
cloud
of breath on the air,

dwell
in our crowded hearts
our steaming bathrooms, kitchens full of
things to be done, the
ordinary streets.

Thrust close your smile
that we know you, terrible joy.[184]

*

This book began in a spirit of play several years ago. It was an invitation to have a dance with the animus while doing something I love, reading and writing poetry. Gradually it began to take on a feeling of importance, as if this little phenomenological exercise ambitiously hoped to become an intellectual landmark.

The intention to share with other women an experience of active imagination threatens to become a lifelong task. Laudable as such an aim may be, should it override other facets of the small gem that is my existence on earth? That feels like an animus aim . . . the fall of the pall of thrall: to feel bound to read everything ever written on the masculine, to trace every reference through its family tree to its ultimate source, true scholarship. Each chapter calls out to be extended and revised again and again. Every example is under surveillance, suspected of bias and inappropriateness. Dozens of poems raise their hands and cry, "Take *me!*"

I laugh about this with women friends, about my compulsion to

---

[184] Ellman and O'Clair, *Norton Anthology,* pp. 1061-1063.

overpaint the portrait. Regina says, "Name it *Animus Aeternus ad infinitum.*" "Or *exterminatus,*" adds Mary. Betty suggests I put my attention on a new project. Trickster says, "Call up a man and ask if you can stop now."

*

Matins. It is my rare day to sleep late, and I waken early with a dream.

O shadow of the authentic! I decide to write rather than go back to sleep; it feels like a masculine decision.

In the dream I am with an attractive man in some mutual endeavor at a Veterans' Hospital. Later we are dancing. It's time to go and we have had a last dance, but impulsively, lovingly, he says, "Just one more . . . ," and we happily fall into each other's arms again, and dance . . .

The authentic, I said. It thrusts up close. Dream images of healing, warriors, physical pleasure and emotional connection after a day of decisions. A day spent keeping myself to the task of pushing through the final writing and decision making on this book, which must be shortened. It feels male, to be pushing, largely from the lower back, while the pressure of concentrated thinking seems to be in my head. But it reminds me of pregnancy and labor.

The poet fondles and breaks the new-laid egg. Culling; what to keep and what to cut? Have I thought this through? Please be clear, that's all He asks! How She hates to cut and excerpt poems! Last-minute misgivings abut my hard-gained opinions. *The zest to follow through.*

Stir the holy grains. Parent-teacher conference. Emotional confrontations with my child. Was ego warranted? Was discipline called for?

The authentic rolls just out of reach. Phone crisis with a patient. What would help? Does she know I hear her? Long-distance call from another daughter, my heart stretched over miles by *her* hard choices.

Tell me, beloved, how to follow. A special report on the evening news about the death penalty. Is killing warranted? Yes, says Justice, through the frightened eyes of an innocent citizen trapped inside like a prisoner and no longer safe on her front porch. No, cries Mercy, through the moustached mouth of a gentle activist on Channel 3.

How to follow through to the country beneath the waves. We are close to war. Is war ever warranted? How did I help create a society which supports sociopaths and sends the capable and competent youth off to feed the minotaur? I don't want my son to go, nor the woman I saw on the news last week, saying good-by to her little children to go to Arabia with her National Guard unit.

You step out of your bones. Winter has come, but the repairman never did, and the window is still broken. I don't want to fix it.

The authentic, I said. Before sleeping I turn on the TV for a minute of relaxation and get a documentary on Vietnam veterans. Almost seduced into watching it, I "just say no" to Post-traumatic Stress Disorder , and now wake up dancing in the psychic vicinity of the V.A. Do we dare to dance?

Marvelous truth, confront us at every turn. My patient was right, the lessons get harder, the choices more difficult, and we are all being peeled like onions.

Thrust close your smile. The eternal masculine . . . how he loves to dance! A new tune is beginning, and we are both in anticipation.

We know you, terrible joy. I dance in his arms, and rest in her bosom.

Terrible joy . . . marvelous truth.

Bibliography

Akhmatova, Anna. *Twenty Poems.* Trans. Jane Kenyon. St. Paul: Eighties Press and Ally Press, 1985.

Bennett, Paula. *My Life a Loaded Gun.* Boston: Beacon Press, 1986.

Binswanger, Hilde, "Positive Aspects of the Animus." *Spring 1963.*

Bly, Robert. "The Descent into Ourselves." Boulder: *Sounds True* Audio Tapes Catalogue, 1989-90.

Bolen, Jean Shinoda. *Goddesses in Everywoman.* New York: Harper and Row, 1984.

_____. *Gods in Everyman: A New Psychology of Men's Lives and Loves.* New York: Harper and Row, 1989.

Bradway, Katherine. "Gender Identity and Gender Roles: Their Place in Analytic Practice." In *Jungian Analysis.* Ed. Murray Stein. Boulder: Shambhala, 1984.

Brooks, Cleanth, and Warren, Robert Penn, eds. *Understanding Poetry.* New York: Holt, Rinehart and Winston, 1976.

Brooks, Gwendolyn. *In the Mecca.* New York: Harper and Row, 1964.

Brown, Malcom. *The Healing Touch: An Introduction to Organismic Psychotherapy.* Mendocino: Life Rhythm, 1990.

Bundtzen, Linda K. *Plath's Incarnations: Woman and the Creative Process.* Ann Arbor: University of Michigan Press, 1983.

Campbell, Camille. *Meditations with Teresa of Avila.* Santa Fe: Bear and Co., 1985.

Claremont de Castillejo, Irene. *Knowing Woman: A Feminine Psychology.* New York: G.P. Putnam's Sons, 1973.

Covington, Coline. "In Search of the Heroine." *Journal of Analytical Psychology,* vol. 34, no. 3 (1989).

Cutts, Christina. "When Logic Fails." *San Francisco Jung Institute Library Journal,* vol. 9, no. 3 (1990).

Dash, Joan. *A Life of One's Own: Three Gifted Women and the Men They Married.* New York: Harper and Row, 1973.

Dickinson, Emily. *The Poems of Emily Dickenson.* 3 vols. Ed. Thomas H. Johnson. Cambridge: Belknap Press, 1955.

Douglas, Claire. *The Woman in the Mirror.* Boston: Sigo Press, 1990.

Ellman, Richard, and O'Clair, Robert, eds. *The Norton Anthology of Modern Poetry.* New York: W.W. Norton and Co., 1973.

Engelman, Joan C. "Beyond the Anima." In *Jung's Challenge to Contemporary Religion*. Ed. Murray Stein and Robert L. Moore. Wilmette, IL: Chiron Publications, 1987.

Fordham, Michael. *Children As Individuals*. New York: Putnam, 1970.

Frank, Elizabeth. *Louise Bogan: A Portrait*. New York: Alfred A. Knopf, 1985.

Galenson, Eleanor, ed. "Psychology of Women." Panel reports in *Journal of the American Psychoanalytic Association*, vol. 24, nos. 1, 3 (1976).

Gilligan, Carol. *In a Different Voice*. Cambridge: Harvard U.P., 1982.

Gimbutas, Marija. *The Language of the Goddess*. New York: Harper and Row, 1989.

Gould, Jean. *Modern American Women Poets*. New York: Dodd, Mead and Co., 1989.

Graves, Robert. *The White Goddess: A Historical Grammar of Poetic Myth*. New York: Farrar, Straus and Giroux, 1948.

H.D. *H.D.: Collected Poems, 1912-1944*. New York: New Directions, 1983.

Hall, James. *Jungian Dream Interpretation: A Handbook of Theory and Practice*. Toronto: Inner City Books.

Hall, Nor. *The Moon and the Virgin*. New York: Haper and Row, 1980.

Hannah, Barbara. *Encounters with the Soul: Active Imagination As Developed by C.G. Jung*. Santa Monica: Sigo Press, 1981.

Harding, M. Esther. *The Way of All Women*. New York: Harper Colophon, 1975.

Hawking, Stephen. *A Brief History of Time*. New York: Bantam, 1988.

Hildegard of Bingen. *Illuminations of Hildegard of Bingen*. With a commentary by Matthew Fox. Santa Fe: Bear and Co., 1985.

Hillman, James. *Anima: An Anatomy of a Personified Notion*. Dallas: Spring Publications, 1976.

Jewett, Julia. "Womansoul: A Feminine Corrective to Christian Imagery." In *Jung's Challenge to Contemporary Religion*. Ed. Murray Stein and Robert L. Moore. Wilmette, IL: Chiron Publications, 1987.

Jung, C.G. *The Collected Works* (Bollingen Series XX). 20 vols. Trans. R.F.C. Hull. Ed. H. Read, M. Fordham, G. Adler, Wm. McGuire. Princeton: Princeton University Press, 1953-1979.

_____. *C.G. Jung Letters* (Bollingen Series XCV). 2 vols. Ed. G. Adler and A. Jaffé. Princeton: Princeton University Press, 1973.

_____. *The Visions Seminars: Notes of the Seminars, 1930-1934*. Zurich: Spring Publications, 1976.

Jung, Emma. *Animus and Anima.* Zurich: Spring Publications, 1957.

Kroll, Judith. *Chapters in Mythology: The Poetry of Sylvia Plath.* New York: Harper and Row, 1976.

Lapp, Claudia E. *Cloud Gate.* Ellicott City, MD: The Muses' Company, 1985.

Lawrence, D.H. *Phantasia of the Unconscious.* London: Penguin Books, 1922 (USA 1977).

Leonard, Linda. *On the Way to the Wedding: Transforming the Love Relationship.* Boston: Shambhala, 1987.

_____. *Witness to the Fire: Creativity and the Veil of Addiction.* Boston: Shambhala, 1989.

Levertov, Denise. *Breathing the Water.* New York: New Directions, 1984.

_____. *Candles in Babylon.* New York: New Directions, 1978.

_____. *Poems: 1960-67.* New York: New Dimensions, 1967.

Mattoon, Mary Ann. *Applied Dream Analysis: A Jungian Approach.* Washington, DC: V.H. Winston and Sons, 1978.

McNeely, Deldon Anne. *Touching: Body Therapy and Depth Psychology.* Toronto: Inner City Books, 1987.

Meier, C.A. *The Meaning and Significance of Dreams.* Boston: Sigo Press, 1987.

Millay, Edna St. Vincent. *Collected Poems.* New York: Harper and Row, 1956.

Moore, Robert, and Gillette, Douglas. *King, Warrior, Magician, Lover: Rediscovering the Archetypes of the Mature Masculine.* New York: Harper and Row, 1990.

Nagy, Marilyn. "Menstruation and Shamanism." In *Betwixt and Between: Patterns of Masculine and Feminine Initiation.* Ed. Louise Mahdi, Steven Foster and Meredith Little. La Salle, IL: Open Court, 1987.

Nathanson, Sue. *Soul Crisis: One Woman's Journey Through Abortion to Renewal.* New York: New American Library, 1989.

Neumann, E. *The Origins and History of Consciousness* (Bollingen Series XLII). Princeton: Princeton University Press, 1971.

_____. "The Psychological Stages of Feminine Development." (First section of *Zur Psychologie des Weiblichen;* Zurich: Rascher Verlag, 1953.) Orig. trans. by Rebecca Jacobson, revised by Hildegard Nagel and Jane Pratt. In *Spring 1959.*

Oliver, Mary. *American Primitive.* Boston: Little, Brown and Co., 1976.

_____. *Dream Work.* Boston: The Atlantic Monthly Press, 1986.

Perera, Sylvia Brinton. *Descent to the Goddess: A Way of Initiation for Women.* Toronto: Inner City Books, 1981.

_____. *The Scapegoat Complex: Toward a Mythology of Shadow and Guilt.* Toronto: Inner City Books, 1986.

Piercy, Marge. *Circles on the Water.* New York: Alfred A. Knopf, 1985.

_____. *The Moon Is Always Female.* New York: Alfred A. Knopf, 1985.

Plath, Sylvia. *Ariel.* New York: Harper and Row, 1961.

_____. *Collected Poems.* New York: Harper and Row, 1981.

_____. *Johnny Panic and the Bible of Dreams.* New York: Harper and Row, 1952.

_____. *The Journals of Sylvia Plath.* Ed. Ted Hughes and Francis McCullough. New York: The Dial Press, 1982.

_____. *Letters Homes: Correspondence 1950-63.* Selected and edited by Aurelia S. Plath. New York: Bantam, 1975.

Rich, Adrienne. *Blood, Bread, and Poetry: Selected Prose, 1979-1985.* New York: W.W. Norton and Co., 1986.

_____. *Diving into the Wreck: Poems 1971-1972.* New York: W.W. Norton and Co., 1969.

_____. *Leaflets: Poems 1965-1968.* New York: W.W. Norton and Co., 1973.

_____. *On Lies, Secrets, and Silence.* New York: W.W. Norton and Co., 1979.

_____. *Sources.* Woodside, CA: The Meyeck Press, 1983.

_____. *Poems: Selected and New, 1950-1974.* New York: W.W. Norton and Co, 1974.

_____. *Of Woman Born: Motherhood As Experience and Institution.* New York: W.W. Norton and Co., 1975.

Samuels, Andrew. *Jung and the Post-Jungians.* London: Routledge and Kegan Paul, 1985.

Sarton, May. *Collected Poems.* New York: W.W. Norton and Co., 1974.

_____. *Halfway to Silence.* New York: W.W. Norton and Co., 1980.

Sharp, Daryl. *Personality Types: Jung's Model of Typology.* Toronto: Inner City Books, 1987.

Singer, June. *Androgyny: Toward a New Theory of Sexuality.* Garden City, NY: Anchor Press/Doubleday, 1976.

Taylor, Glenda. *Life Is a River.* Nacogdoches, TX: Hawkins Publishing Co., 1984.

Tepperman, Jean. "Witch." In *No More Masks: An Anthology of Poems by Women.* Ed. Florence Howe and Ellen Bass. New York: The Anchor Press, 1973.

Teresa of Avila. *Meditations with Teresa of Avila.* Preface and Versions by Camille Anne Campbell. Santa Fe: Bear and Co., 1985.

Thomas, Dylan. *Collected Poems.* New York: New Directions, 1971.

Tiger, Madeline. "Older Brothers." In *Ikon,* 2nd series, no. 8 (1988).

von Franz, Marie-Louise. *Puer Aeternus: A Psychological Study of the Adult Struggle with the Paradise of Childhood.* 2nd ed. Santa Monica: Sigo Press, 1981.

_____. "The Process of Individuation." In *Man and His Symbols.* Ed. C.G. Jung. New York: Dell Publishing Co., 1968.

_____. *Shadow and Evil in Fairytales.* Zurich: Spring Publications, 1974.

Wehr, Demaris S. *Jung and Feminism.* Boston: Beacon Press, 1987.

Wheelwright, Jane. *For Women Growing Older.* Houston: C.G. Jung Educational Center, 1984.

Whitmont, Edward C. *Return of the Goddess.* New York: Crossroad, 1982.

Winnicott, D.W. *The Maturational Process and the Facilitating Environment.* New York: International University Press, 1965.

Woodman, Marion. *Addiction to Perfection: The Still Unravished Bride.* Toronto: Inner City Books, 1982.

_____. *The Owl Was a Baker's Daughter: Obesity, Anorexia Nervosa and the Repressed Feminine.* Toronto: Inner City Books, 1980.

_____. *The Pregnant Virgin: A Process of Psychological Transformation.* Toronto: Inner City Books, 1985.

_____. *The Ravaged Bridegroom: Masculinity in Women.* Toronto: Inner City Books, 1990.

Woolf, Virginia. *The Death of the Moth and Other Essays.* New York: Harcourt Brace Jovanovich, 1942.

_____. *Moments of Being.* New York: Harcourt Brace Jovanovich, 1976.

Young-Eisendrath, Polly. *Hags and Heroes: A Feminist Approach to Jungian Psychotherapy with Couples.* Toronto: Inner City Books, 1984.

Young-Eisendrath, Polly, and Wiedemann, Florence. *Female Authority: Empowering Women Through Psychotherapy.* New York: Guilford Press, 1987.

Index

Gesell, Arnold, 60
Gilligan, Carol, 23n, 60
Gimbutas, Marija, 50-51
"Girl in White" (Piercy), 103
Goddess, Great, 48-52, 54-56, 69-70
God-images, 47-48, 51-55, 69-70
"good-enough" mother, 25, 143
Goodyear, Gayonne, 7
Graves, Robert, 54
Great Mother, 21, 86
"Guest, The" (Akhmatova), 129
"Gypsy Desire" (Bucy), 159

H.D., 135
Hades, 69, 106
hair, cutting off, 75
Hall, Nor, 143n, 172n
"Hanging Man, The" (Plath), 96
Harding, M. Esther, 173n
Hawking, Stephen, 167
Hecate, 90
Hephaestus, 69
Hera, 90
hermaphroditism, 22-23, 25, 27, 144
Hermes, 54, 69
hero/heroine, 66-67, 82, 86-88, 109,
    117, 136, 139, 146-147, 152,
    154n, 166
Hestia, 172
hetaira, 118
Hildegard of Bingen, 7, 15
Hillman, James, 15, 45n, 132, 154n
Horney, Karen, 63
Hughes, Ted, 92, 94-95, 98-99

"I Am a Light You Could Read By"
    (Piercy), 149
"I Would Have It" (Taylor), 39
idealization, 136, 140-141
identification, 61-62, 66, 139, 143
"Illustrious Ancestors" (Levertov), 164
In a Different Voice, 23n, 60
"In Honor of That Not Spoken" (Taylor),
    16-17
"In Mind" (Levertov), 84
incest, 129-131
individuation, 9, 13, 21-23, 32-33, 48,
    52, 59, 64-65, 109, 146, 149, 155
inflation, 45, 48, 77, 117

integration, 21-25, 52, 62, 66, 73, 152
introversion, 81, 155
"Invocation to Kali" (Sarton), 56-57
Ishtar, 54
Isis, 54

Jesus, 69
Jewett, Julia, 172n
Jung, C.G., 9, 11-12, 21, 23, 29-33,
    45n, 58, 60-64, 98, 139, 152n
Jung, Emma, 63, 145-146
"Jung" (Lapp), 12

Kali, 56, 90
"King Friday," 156, 161
Klein, Melanie, 60, 63
Kohlberg, Lawrence, 60
Kore, 103, 147
Krishna, 69
Kroll, Judith, 98

"Lady Lazarus" (Plath), 91
"Laocoon Is the Name of the Figure"
    (Piercy), 108
Lapp, Claudia E., 12, 29, 111, 163
Lawrence, D.H., 71
Leonard, Linda, 67, 143n, 173n
Levertov, Denise, 27, 36-37, 84, 164,
    168-169, 174-179
Lindsey, Karen, 92n
"Lines Written in Recapitulation"
    (Millay), 38
"Little Exercise" (Bishop), 55
"Living in Sin" (Rich), 148-149
Loevinger, Jane, 63-65, 116-117
Logos, 11, 13, 28, 32, 64, 73, 145
Lorde, Audre, 92n
"Lullabye" (Sexton), 112

Madonna, 47, 49-50, 87
"Magi" (Plath), 96
Mahler, Margaret, 63
Mann, Rachel Eliza, 35
masculine *(see also* father archetype/
    complex), 21-23, 30-40, 44, 49,
    52, 59-60, 62, 73, 82-83, 88, 92-
    93, 106, 108-111, 115-135, 146,
    156-172
Maslow, Abraham, 60

Marie-Louise von Franz, Honorary Patron

Studies in Jungian Psychology
by Jungian Analysts

Sewn Paperbacks

MARION WOODMAN (Toronto)
Addiction to Perfection: The Still Unravished Bride. 208pp. $17
Deluxe hard-cover edition: $22
A powerful and authoritative look at the psychology of modern women. Examines dreams, mythology, food rituals, body imagery, sexuality and creativity. Illus.

The Pregnant Virgin: Psychological Transformation. 208pp. $17
Deluxe hard-cover edition: $22
A celebration of the feminine in both sexes. Explores the wisdom of the body in eating disorders, relationships, dreams, addictions, etc. Illustrated.

The Ravaged Bridegroom: Masculinity in Women. 224pp. $18
Breaks new ground exploring the psychological impact of patriarchy. Reveals the creative potential of a revitalized masculinity in both men and women. Illustrated.

DELDON ANNE MCNEELY (Lynchburg, VA)
Touching: Body Therapy and Depth Psychology. 128pp. $14
Illustrates how these two disciplines, both concerned with restoring life to an ailing human psyche, may be integrated in theory and practice.

DARYL SHARP (Toronto)
Personality Types: Jung's Model of Typology. 128pp. $14
Comprehensive presentation of Jung's views on introversion, extraversion and the four functions he called a psychological "compass." Illustrative diagrams.

SYLVIA BRINTON PERERA (New York)
Descent to the Goddess: Way of Initiation for Women. 112pp. $14
Provocative study of the need for an inner, female authority in a masculine-oriented society. Rich in insights from dreams, myth and the author's practice.

POLLY YOUNG-EISENDRATH (Philadelphia)
Hags and Heroes: A Feminist Approach to Jungian Psychotherapy with Couples. 192pp. $16
Emphasis on the feminine principle and reassessing the nature of female authority in relationships. Helpful guidelines for both therapists and clients.

NANCY QUALLS-CORBETT (Birmingham)
The Sacred Prostitute: Eternal Aspect of the Feminine. 176pp. $16
Shows how our vitality depends on rediscovering the ancient connection between spirituality and physical love. Illustrated. *(Foreword by Marion Woodman.)*

Prices and payment (check or money order) in $U.S. (in Canada, $Cdn)

Add Postage/Handling: 1-2 books, $2; 3-4 books, $4; 5-8 books, $7

Complete Catalogue and SAMPLER free on request

INNER CITY BOOKS
Box 1271, Station Q, Toronto, Canada M4T 2P4
Tel. (416) 927-0355